Comprehension

grades 3-5

D0771923

One 15-Minute Comprehension Builder for Every Week of the School Year

Features a wide range of read-aloud stories with comprehension questions

- Adventure
- Animal
- Folktale
- Historical

- Humor
- Realistic Fiction
- Suspense
- Fantasy

Managing Editor: Debra Liverman

Editorial Team: Becky S. Andrews, Kimberley Bruck, Karen P. Shelton, Diane Badden, Amy Payne, Karen A. Brudnak, Sarah Hamblet, Hope Rodgers, Dorothy C. McKinney

Production Team: Lisa K. Pitts, Pam Crane, Rebecca Saunders, Jennifer Cappoen, Chris Curry, Theresa Lewis Goode, Ivy L. Koonce, Clint Moore, Greg D. Rieves, Barry Slate, Donna K. Teal, Zane Williard, Tazmen Carlisle, Irene Harvley-Felder, Amy Kirtley-Hill, Kristy Parton, Debbie Shoffner, Cathy Edwards Simrell, Lynette Dickerson, Mark Rainey

Social Stud

www.themailbox.com

Table of Contents

How to Use

Using *Listening Comprehension* is easy. Just follow these simple steps:

1. Pick a story.

2. Prepare students to listen.
- Introduce and discuss the highlighted vocabulary words.
- Invite students to make predictions. Use the story's title, genre, or illustration to involve students in a discussion about what might happen in the story.

3. Read the story aloud.

4. Check for comprehension.
Discuss the comprehension questions at the end of the story with students or have them write their answers to one or more questions.

For other quick and easy assessments, ask students to
- summarize the story orally or in writing
- illustrate the story
- identify meanings of key words
- list three things they've learned
- identify the story's genre
- list significant details from the story
- list three key qualities of a character

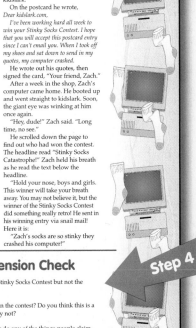

Step 1

Step 2

Step 4

The Stinky Socks Contest
by Kim T. Griswell

Zach keyed in the address of his favorite Web site. When the page finished loading, the familiar giant eye greeted him with a wink. Zach winked back.

"Hey, dude! What do you have for me today?" Zach asked.

Zach's favorite dotcom featured weekly contests that kids could enter to win cool prizes. Last week a boy from Australia won a computer by naming the capital of every South American country. The week before, a girl from India wrote a poem that won her an all-expenses-paid trip to the theme park of her choice.

He clicked on the lime green contest button and held his breath. A wriggling giant sock came up on the screen. The headline read "Announcing the World's First Stinky Socks Contest!" Zach **scanned** the rules. Entry was open to kids between the ages of eight and 13. In order to win, contestants had to prove their socks were the stinkiest on the planet by sending in a quote from someone who had smelled them. All entries had to be received by midnight in exactly two weeks.

"Whoopee!" Zach shouted as he closed the **browser.** Finally, a contest he could win!

His best friend, Derrick, helped him plan his **strategy.** First, he'd wear the same socks every day for a week. Then he'd take his shoes off in public places and write down whatever comments people made. Someone was bound to say something that would make Zach a winner!

Zach's feet must have been **prime** stinkers because he got his first comment after only two days.

"Zach?" his mom asked when he took his shoes off to watch television. "When is the last time you changed your socks?"

Zach grinned. "I can't change my socks, Mom. I'm in a contest."

"What kind of a contest?" she said, giving him that "here we go again" look.

"A stinky socks contest!"

Zach's mom shook her head. "Well, you win. Go change your socks."

"No, Mom. Really. It's on kidslark.com. First prize is a dirt bike!"

"Zach, if your feet get much worse, Barney will faint!"

Barney was their three-year-old Rottweiler. He was sitting across the room from Zach with his nose tucked under his paw.

Zach laughed. "Good one, Barney!"

He grabbed his journal and wrote down the quote: "Zach's socks are so stinky they could make a Rottweiler faint!"

His next chance for a quote came at the Rock and Roll Burger Barn. When the waitress came to take his order, Zach slipped off his right shoe and waved his foot around.

"Honey," the waitress said, looking down her nose at him. "I hate to be rude, but those socks smell so bad they could wake Elvis from the dead."

"Yes!" Zach stuck his foot back in his shoe and wrote the quote in his journal.

On Saturday, Zach went to Derrick's birthday party. As Derrick's mom passed around plates heaped with chocolate cake and **Neapolitan** ice cream, Zach took off his shoes. Megan Schwartz scrunched up her face. "Mrs. Russell? Make Zach put his shoes back on. His stinky socks are melting my ice cream!"

Zach winked at Derrick. Derrick **glared.** "Not here, Zach. It's my birthday."

Before he put his shoes back on, Zach wrote down the quote.

By the end of the week, he had plenty of great stinky socks quotes. He kicked off his shoes and sat down in front of his computer. He tapped out a rhythm on the desktop as he waited for the Web page to load. When the giant eye winked at him, Zach clicked on the Enter Contest Now button. He filled out the entry form and carefully typed his quotes in the box provided. Then, just as he was about to click on the send button, the screen froze.

"No!" Zach moaned. "Not now!"

He **rebooted** his computer, but instead of the usual smiling computer **icon,** a frowning computer appeared on his desktop. No amount of **trouble-shooting** would make the computer icon smile again. Zach's machine would have to go into the shop.

Zach couldn't believe his luck. After all that work! He might as well forget the contest. Forget the bike. He'd never win now.

Then Zach remembered some-thing. **email** wasn't the only way to someone. He could send a postcard! He still had three days until the contest ended. That should be enough time for the card to reach kidslark.

On the postcard he wrote,

Dear kidslark.com,

I've been working hard all week to win your Stinky Socks Contest. I hope that you will accept this postcard entry since I can't email you. When I took off my shoes and sat down to send in my quotes, my computer crashed.

He wrote out his quotes, then signed the card, "Your friend, Zach."

After a week in the shop, Zach's computer came home. He booted up and went straight to kidslark. Soon, the giant eye was winking at him once again.

"Hey, dude!" Zach said. "Long time, no see."

He scrolled down the page to find out who had won the contest. The headline read "Stinky Socks Catastrophe!" Zach held his breath as he read the text below the headline.

"Hold your nose, boys and girls. This winner will take your breath away. You may not believe it, but the winner of the Stinky Socks Contest did something really retro! He sent in his winning entry via snail mail! Here it is:

"Zach's socks are so stinky they crashed his computer!"

🔲 Comprehension Check

1. Why does Zach think he can win the Stinky Socks Contest but not the others he mentions?

2. What is Zach and Derrick's plan to win the contest? Do you think this is a contest-winning strategy? Why or why not?

3. Do you think stinky socks could really do any of the things people claim Zach's socks do? Why or why not?

4. Zach wears the same socks and takes off his shoes in public places to win the Stinky Socks Contest. What would you be willing to do to win a contest?

The Lucky Cap

by Kim T. Griswell

Dirk awakened to bright blue skies, but things had changed by the time school got out. Back in his room, he dropped his backpack on the floor and grabbed his favorite cap from the bedpost. His father had given him that cap. His dad called it his lucky cap because he'd been wearing it the year his team crossed the finish line first in the California Coastal **Marathon.**

Dirk jammed the sea-blue cap over his dark, **springy** hair and yelled to his mom, "I'm heading down to the beach!"

"Be back before suppertime!" she called back.

He stomped his foot down on the tail of his skateboard to make it pop up. Then he caught the nose with his right hand. When he got outside, he put the board down and skated along the sidewalk.

As he reached the main road, he turned south into the wind. Dust and litter blew around and past him. Weird weather, he thought. Then he turned the corner and the full force of the wind hit him. Dirk nearly fell off his skateboard as he grabbed for his cap.

What is going on? Dirk wondered.

He shoved his cap down more firmly on his head and kicked toward the **pier.** Wind howled beneath it. A couple of elderly crabbers leaned over the rail, pulling at one of the crab lines and yelling. They were there every day, pulling in a few crabs.

Then it happened. A gust of wind whipped beneath Dirk's cap and blew it off his head.

"No!" Dirk yelled as he skidded to a stop. The cap skipped along the pier toward the rail. He had to catch it before another gust tossed it over the rail and into the ocean.

As he reached the crabbers, he froze. His heart started to pound as he saw what they were yelling about. A little girl had gone over the rail. The wind couldn't be that strong, could it? She clung to one of the crab lines, screaming at the top of her lungs. The crabbers were struggling to pull her up.

Dirk's cap blew farther away from him. He took another step toward it. As he did, one of the men's hands slipped on the line and the rope dropped back a foot. The man turned and yelled to Dirk for help. Dirk realized he'd have to choose: his dad's lucky cap or the girl.

Dirk **hesitated** for only a moment. Then he turned away from the cap, grabbed the line, and pulled. With Dirk's help, they hauled the girl up. Once they had her back to safety, Dirk looked up and down the pier, hoping to see

his cap. No such luck.

He turned toward the water. Whitecaps raced along the water, pushing the cap before them. His dad's lucky cap was headed out to sea. What would his dad say when he told him he'd lost his cap?

Then someone tugged at his hand. He looked down. The little girl looked up at him. Big tears were spilling down her cheeks. "Thanks." She sniffed. "You saved me."

Dirk shrugged. "Hey, no problem. Just lucky I was here to help, I guess," he said as her parents raced toward them.

He glanced back at the ocean. Suddenly, he realized that if his cap hadn't blown off when it did, he'd have skated past the men on the pier. Dirk grinned. He knew exactly what his dad would say when he told him what had happened. That was one lucky cap!

Comprehension Check

1. Why is the cap special to Dirk's dad?

2. Why couldn't the crabbers pull the little girl to safety without Dirk's help?

3. What role did the weather play in this story?

4. Have you ever chosen to give up something important to you to help someone else? Explain.

Swamp Stories

by Nancy J. Cavanaugh

"Mom, Robby and I are going for a walk!" Jim yelled.

"Okay, but stay within sight of the campground," Mom warned.

"We will," Jim said.

But somehow they got turned around. Now Jim and his younger brother stood close together, surrounded by the tall **cypress** trees and short **saw palmettos** of the Okefenokee Swamp. Jim wasn't sure he could find their campsite again, and the sun was already dipping toward the treetops.

"Do you hear that splashing sound?" Robby asked.

"Yeah," Jim answered.

"Remember that story Uncle Owen told us?" Robby asked.

"Which one?" Jim asked. Uncle Owen had more stories than a library.

"The one about those alligators wrestling in the swamp," Robby said.

"Oh, Robby, stop worrying about alligators," Jim said.

Their Uncle Owen was born and raised in the Okefenokee Swamp, so he told lots of swamp stories. The stories usually scared Robby, but he always begged for more.

They heard more splashing, and Robby's eyes grew wider.

"C'mon, Jim," Robby pleaded. "Let's go back."

"Okay, okay. We will," Jim said, not wanting Robby to know that they might be lost.

Jim walked toward the splashing sound. He knew that if they found the river, they had a better chance of finding their way back.

"Don't go that way!" Robby exclaimed.

"We have to," Jim insisted, grabbing his little brother's hand.

Jim was a little nervous, but he was pretty sure the splashing wasn't alligators wrestling. At least he hoped it wasn't.

When they got to the water, they realized that the sound came from fish jumping.

"See, Robby?" Jim said. "It's just fish. Remember Uncle Owen told us that when he was little, there were so many fish in the swamp that they used to jump into his boat?"

"Uh-huh," Robby answered.

As the two boys made their way up the river, Jim searched for things that looked familiar. He hoped they were going the right way because it was starting to get dark.

As they came to a bend in the river, Jim saw hundreds of floating objects in the water. Another Uncle Owen story came to mind.

"The gators were so thick," Uncle Owen had once told him, "it looked like you could walk on 'em like steppin'-stones and get all the way across the lake."

Earlier that day, the park ranger at their campground had told them, "If you see an alligator, keep your distance. Don't bother it, and it won't bother you." Jim wondered what the ranger would say about seeing *hundreds* of alligators.

"Jim!" Robby pointed toward the water. "Look at all those lily pads!"

Relief washed over Jim. They were lily pads, not alligators! In the swamp's dark shadows, Jim's eyes were playing tricks on him.

"How many do you think there are?" Robby asked.

"More than a hundred," Jim answered, thankful to be talking about lily pads instead of alligators.

Jim's relief didn't last long. This part of the river didn't look familiar at all. They really were lost. Now what?

He looked **skyward.** When would the moon rise? If they followed the moon, it might lead them to their campsite. Still, he hoped they were sitting by the campfire roasting marshmallows by the time the moon rose high enough to guide them.

"C'mon, Robby," he said.

The two boys went farther upstream until they saw a path. That's when things began looking familiar again.

After walking a few feet up the path, the boys heard a loud slap.

Robby froze in his tracks. "Do you know what that sounded like?" he asked.

"What?" Jim asked.

"Remember that mosquito-catching alligator Uncle Owen told us about?" Robby asked. "The one that held its mouth open until mosquitoes covered its tongue and then snapped its mouth shut?"

Slap! The sound came again.

Jim was scared, but he had a feeling they were close to their campsite. He grabbed Robby's hand again and kept going. His heart pounded as he waited for the next slap. After a few minutes, they came to the end of the path and entered a clearing. Slap! Jim saw what was making the slapping sound—a window flap on their pop-up camper. They had found their way back to camp!

"We were just starting to get worried," Mom said.

"Everything okay?" Dad asked.

"It is now," Jim said. As he stuck another log on the campfire, he thought about the stories he could tell that evening. Now Uncle Owen wasn't the only one with swamp stories to tell.

Comprehension Check

1. Why does Uncle Owen have so many swamp stories?

2. What does Jim think he sees floating in the open water? What does it turn out to be?

3. Do you think it is safe for Jim and Robby to leave their campsite by themselves? Why or why not?

4. Do you have a storyteller like Uncle Owen in your family? If so, what types of stories does he or she like to tell?

Hothead

by Constance Faye Mudore

The moment she kicked the ball, Lindsey knew it was going to land in Mrs. Mudgeon's yard. She groaned. The elderly woman had warned Lindsey and her friends that the next time the ball entered her yard, she would keep it. Sure enough, Mrs. Mudgeon, followed by her **pug,** Max, scurried out and scooped up the ball.

"This is mine now!" she shouted over the fence.

Terry, who had been playing ball with Lindsey, muttered, "That lady must have some kind of soccer ball radar. What are we going to do now?"

The ball was Lindsey's. She yelled, "You can't keep it. It belongs to me!"

"Not anymore!" Mrs. Mudgeon yelled back.

Lindsey screamed, "You're a mean woman. I'll report you to the police for stealing!"

"Well, of all the nerve!" replied Mrs. Mudgeon. Clutching the ball, she stomped into the house and slammed the door. Max stayed outside and barked at them.

"You're such a **hothead**," said Terry. "You'll never get the ball back now."

"Thanks for backing me up," said Lindsey.

"Face it, Lindsey. When things don't go your way, you blow up. She might have returned it if you hadn't gotten mad."

"If you're so smart, why didn't you do something?" Lindsey shouted.

"Now you're yelling at me!" Terry said. "Good luck getting your ball

back." He turned and left.

Lindsey was now so angry she howled in rage. Terry did not turn around. On her way home, Lindsey didn't notice how the sunlight turned rosy as it **filtered** through the autumn maples lining the street. She was thinking about Mrs. Mudgeon.

The entire neighborhood knew that the elderly woman was **cranky** and kept to herself. She lived alone and rarely went outside, except when kids showed up to play on the **vacant** lot that bordered her property. Then she stood on her porch and hollered when the ball came into her yard.

Anyone who lives next to a vacant lot ought to get used to the fact that kids are going to play there, thought Lindsey. Unfortunately, Mrs. Mudgeon never had. "Go play in the park!" she would yell. But the park was six blocks away. Why couldn't Mrs. Mudgeon understand?

When she got home, her mother said, "I just got off the phone with Mrs. Mudgeon. Care to tell me your side?"

Lindsey immediately lost her temper and started shouting about how unfair Mrs. Mudgeon was. Her mother interrupted. "Lindsey, you seem to think it's okay to get angry when things don't go your way. You're mistaken. Tomorrow is Saturday. I want you to go to Mrs. Mudgeon's in the morning and apologize."

Lindsey couldn't believe her ears. Was her mother serious?

The answer was yes. After breakfast the next morning, Lindsey's mother reminded her about visiting

Mrs. Mudgeon. As she headed toward the elderly woman's house, Lindsey walked slowly, then picked up speed. "Might as well get this over with," she said.

When Lindsey arrived at Mrs. Mudgeon's, she knocked on the front door. No one answered. She rang the doorbell. Still no answer. Lindsey grew **impatient**. She tried the door but it was locked. Max came to the window, but instead of barking as usual, he whined and scratched at the glass.

That's odd, thought Lindsey. Maybe she's in the back. If I don't get this over with, mom will send me here again later. She went around and knocked on the back door. Then she heard what sounded like groaning.

"Mrs. Mudgeon? Are you there?" Lindsey shouted.

A small, shaky voice said, "I've fallen. My oven is on, and I can't get to it. I think something is burning."

Lindsey tried the door. It was locked. "Can you open the door?" Lindsey asked.

"No," Mrs. Mudgeon replied. "Don't worry. I'll get help!"

Lindsey ran to the closest house and pounded on the door. "Mrs. Mudgeon has fallen. There might be a fire in her house. Get help!"

Firefighters came quickly and rescued Mrs. Mudgeon. There was no fire, just some burned cookies. The elderly woman had fallen and broken her ankle. An ambulance took her to the hospital.

On Sunday, Lindsey sat in Mrs. Mudgeon's kitchen eating cookies that hadn't burned. She was drinking milk when Mrs. Mudgeon returned her ball.

"Sorry I was rude," **stammered** Lindsey.

Mrs. Mudgeon said, "Sometimes I have trouble with my temper too."

"I guess we have the same problem," Lindsey said with a smile.

"Let's work on it together," Mrs. Mudgeon said, smiling back.

They raised their glasses of milk, clinked them together, and both ate another cookie.

Comprehension Check

1. Why does Lindsey think Mrs. Mudgeon should not be upset when she and her friends kick their ball into the elderly woman's yard?

2. Why do Lindsey's mother and Terry think Lindsey has a problem with her temper?

3. What might Lindsey have done to prevent having a problem with Mrs. Mudgeon?

4. What problem do Lindsey and Mrs. Mudgeon have in common? How might they help one another?

The Mysterious Trail

by Natasha Wing

It was the first time since Ryan's dad died that he had gone anywhere with Brad. Ryan wanted to get away from the house, so they strapped on their helmets and riding gloves, then mounted their mountain bikes. They raced up the side of the hill and found a trail in the woods.

They rode through puddles, around rocks, and across streams. At a flat, shady spot they skidded to a halt. Both boys took swigs of water from their water bottles.

"Let's see where we are," said Brad, snapping his bottle shut. He tucked it back in its rack, then pulled a map out of his backpack and unfolded it. Ryan took his map out too. It was yellow and soft from being folded and unfolded so many times.

"Looks like we're a mile in," said Brad, pointing to a spot on his map. "What trail do you want to take?"

"Let's take Getaway," said Ryan.

"Where do you see that?" asked Brad.

"Here." Ryan pushed his map across Brad's handlebars and pointed to the trail.

"That's not on my map," said Brad. "Where did you get this old thing anyway?"

"My mom was cleaning my dad's closet, and there was a box of stuff in there," Ryan said. "This is a map he drew. He used to come back here when he was a kid."

Brad said, "Sorry about your dad. He was a great guy."

Ryan looked away, blinking. "Thanks," he said. "I miss him. The way he used to play ball with me, take me camping, watch out for me."

Brad nodded. "Yeah. I know."

The boys rode their bikes on the path to where Getaway should have begun. Instead of a trail, they found **scrubby** bushes and twisted vines. The **stub** of a rotted wooden post **jutted** out of one of the bushes.

"Do you think this is it?" asked Brad.

"Let's check it out," said Ryan. "We can always turn back if you get scared." He shot Brad a crooked grin.

"Me? I'm not scared," said Brad. In one motion he pointed his front wheel toward the bushes, hopped on the pedals, and pushed ahead of Ryan. Ryan jolted into action, and off he went after Brad down the mysterious trail.

The trees thickened and formed a **canopy** overhead that nearly blocked out the sun. Brad and Ryan took it slow, bumping over rocks and swishing past jutting branches. Pretty soon, Ryan had worked up a sweat, and Brad's brow had **furrowed** into a deep frown.

"I can't see the trail anymore," Brad said. "I think we're lost."

Ryan stood up on his pedals, looking ahead. As he did, his front tire hit a sharp rock. The rubber exploded with a loud pop. Ryan toppled over the handlebars, landing with a thud that burst the air from his lungs.

Brad skidded to a halt. "You okay?" He dropped his bike and hurried back.

Ryan groaned as he rose to his elbows. "Yeah. But my bike's not."

He pointed to his shredded front tire.

"Oh, no!" Brad poked at the **puncture,** trying to tuck the rubber back in place.

Neither boy wanted to think about how long it would take them

3 1833 05024 0917

to get home with Ryan dragging his bike. The sun had already **crested** and begun to sink toward the hills. What they had thought was a trail had turned into a rock- and vine-strewn jumble that looked exactly like everything around it. It would be hard enough to find their way back in broad daylight, but after dark? Ryan's mouth set in a thin line of worry. They might not find their way out at all. If only his dad were around to help. But he wasn't. He would never be around to watch over him again.

Ryan's chest felt heavy as he brushed himself off and lifted his bike out of the dust.

"Before I fell, I spotted a clearing up ahead," he said. "Let's stop there and get our **bearings.**"

Brad nodded his agreement. They picked their way around boulders and bushes, trying not to lose sight of the clearing.

"Check it out!" shouted Brad when he entered the clearing.

When Ryan caught up, Brad pointed to a weather-beaten clubhouse tucked under a sprawling oak tree. The front door hung crookedly on its hinge.

"Let's see what's inside," said Ryan.

They propped their bikes against the bushes, then walked over to the clubhouse and peered at the faded sign posted on the door.

It read, "Getaway. Keep out by order of Wayne Wilkins."

"That's my dad!" said Ryan. "This must have been his clubhouse when he was a kid."

"That explains the map," said Brad.

The boys pulled open the creaky door and went inside the dark, spiderweb-infested room.

"Look!" said Ryan. "A bike."

In one corner leaned a rusted old bike that at one time had been red.

"This is so **retro,**" said Brad. "No gears, **derailleurs** for shifting, or shocks. And get a load of this coaster brake system. You had to pedal back-ward to stop this thing."

Ryan was quiet. He wiped dirt off the seat with his sweat towel.

"What's up?" asked Brad.

"I'm picturing my dad as a kid riding around on these trails, just like we're doing."

"Hey!" Brad said. "You can ride your dad's bike home. I've got a pump."

After Brad pumped up the tires, Ryan test-rode the bike around the clubhouse. The brakes worked fine.

"I'll put my bike in the clubhouse for now. We can come back with a new tire."

"I guess your dad saved the day," said Brad.

The heaviness began to lift from Ryan's chest. He smiled. "He must still be watching out for me."

Comprehension Check

1. Where does Ryan get his old map?

2. What clue makes the boys think they've found the beginning of the Getaway trail?

3. Why are the two boys so worried when Ryan's bike gets a flat tire?

4. What makes Ryan think his father is still watching out for him?

Gold Rush Days

by Kim T. Griswell

The air was hot, as dry and **raspy** as a sheet of sandpaper. Miguel scrambled through the stiff, golden grass waving its prickly fingers in the afternoon breeze. Hong had already reached the crest of the hill and was beginning to jog toward the stream. Miguel hurried to catch up.

"Are you sure this is the place?" Miguel said.

Hong pointed toward a spot where the stream curled around a tree. "Right there," he said.

"And you're sure it was gold?"

Hong shrugged. "It looked like gold to me. Little yellow flakes down in the sand."

As they broke through the brush near the stream's edge, Miguel whacked into something. He rubbed his throbbing knee as he pulled back a scraggly bush.

"Hong! Look at this!"

He pointed to a weathered sign with a faded **claim** scrawled across it. "Keep away! Private claim!"

"So what?" Hong shrugged.

"So there are still claims on this river." Miguel glanced around nervously. "Some of the **prospectors** out here are pretty wacky. I hear they set traps and even go after people who mess with their claims."

Hong waved his worries away. "That sign's probably left over from the gold rush."

Miguel and Hong worked side by side. Sweat dripped from their bangs and salted their eyes as they dipped their metal pie pans into the clear stream. They scooped up sand and water, then swished it gently, letting it slosh over the lips of the pans. Miguel squinted. Tiny gold flakes sparkled among the grains of sand.

"You see that?" He poked a finger at the flakes.

"I've got some too!" Hong nodded toward his pan.

They were so busy comparing finds, they didn't notice the crackle of twigs and swish of the underbrush parting behind them until a **gruff** voice spoke.

"What are you kids doing out here?" A long-haired man dressed like a **hippie** from the 1960s emerged from the woods. His bell-bottom jeans were stained with mud.

The boys jolted to their feet. Sand and gold dust flew everywhere. The peace signs painted on the man's blue denim jacket did nothing to still the **hammering** of Miguel's heart.

"Nothing! W-we were just leaving!" he stuttered.

They held onto their pie pans like they were life jackets as they made their way across the creek, trying to put as much space between themselves and the nutty-looking prospector as they could. Their shoes were soaked and the legs of their pants dripping as they began to climb the crumbling slope on the other side of the creek.

"Miguel?" Hong whispered. "Do you think he's gonna come after us?"

Miguel glanced back over his shoulder. The man had **hunkered** down by the stream and watched them climb.

"I don't know. Just climb faster," Miguel said.

Sharp pieces of **shale** sliced his fingers and tumbled down the slope behind him as he climbed. When he reached the top, he hoisted Hong up beside him. Then he looked around.

They'd come to the stream via a few rolling hills that bordered the highway. From there, it was a short hike back to town. But on this side, the hills continued to rise, tier after tier of sharp, spiked slopes jutting toward the blue sky. The bottoms of the slopes were littered with scree—pebbles and bits of broken shale that looked like an **avalanche** just waiting to happen.

"We're gonna have to go back across the stream," Hong said. His skin had paled.

Miguel nodded. "But first let's figure out a way to make sure he doesn't see us."

They put their heads together and came up with a plan. First, they **dislodged** enough rocks from the nearest slope to start a slide. Then they tossed their pans into the mix and scrambled out of the way. Dirt and rocks ripped loose and pelted toward the creek below, throwing up a huge cloud of dust.

Crawling on their bellies, they edged close enough to see the prospector's reaction. Shielding his eyes from the sun, he watched the pie pans bob downstream. With a shake of his head, he hurried along the bank after them.

"It worked!" Miguel said.

They kept low as they headed upstream, looking for a place where trees would hide their progress. When they found one, they crept down the slope, then eased into the water. On the opposite bank, they stayed low to the ground and moved as quiet as foxes through the brush. Miguel's knees began to throb and he wanted nothing more than to stand up, but he didn't dare. Just as he thought they might make it, he came nose to wood with a familiar-looking weathered sign.

"Hong!" he whispered. "We must have circled back to where we started."

As the words left his lips, the aging hippie shoved through the bushes nearby.

"Run!" Hong shouted, but Miguel's stiff legs wouldn't obey his commands.

"Are you kids crazy, or what?" the man asked. "I thought you'd drowned!"

"Please, mister, don't hurt us! We're not trying to jump your claim!" Miguel creaked to his feet with his hands up.

The man frowned. "I'm not going to hurt anyone."

"Then why were you following us?" asked Miguel.

"To make sure you guys stayed safe. There are dangerous things out here," the man said, "like mountain lions and **grizzlies.**"

Hong glared at Miguel.

Miguel grinned **sheepishly.** "I guess you were right," he said. "The gold rush is over."

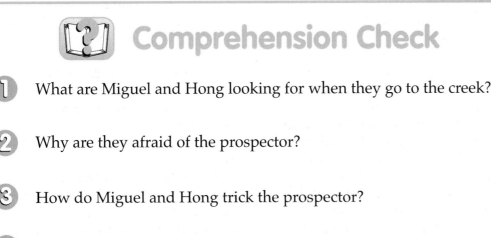

Comprehension Check

1. What are Miguel and Hong looking for when they go to the creek?

2. Why are they afraid of the prospector?

3. How do Miguel and Hong trick the prospector?

4. Why does the prospector follow Miguel and Hong?

Red Squirrel Escape

by Martha Shaffer Campbell

How Red wanted to escape! He wanted to be free again. He could see the spruce trees from his cage, and he remembered days of playing in them with his two brothers and his sister.

Red was a wild squirrel who'd been captured by a man who wanted to tame him. The man, Mr. Cooper, was nice, but he didn't understand that squirrels need their freedom. Red had been born in a hole near the top of a tall spruce stump in a forest close to Mr. Cooper's house.

As soon as Red was able to climb up to the top of the hole and look out, he longed to climb the trees. His bigger brother made the jump first. He sprang from the top of the stump to a nearby spruce tree, just as he'd seen his mother do. Then Red jumped, but he missed and tumbled down to the ground below. He wasn't injured, but he was frightened. He scampered back up the spruce stump and popped into the hole with his heart thumping wildly. He rested for a few minutes; then he came out to try again.

Red's mother jumped back and forth from the tree to the spruce trunk, encouraging him to try again. His brother watched from the tree. Finally, Red jumped. His long toes sank into the bark of the tree. He hung on tightly. He had made it!

His brother chased him up the tree, around the tree, down the tree, and up the tree again. Around and around they went. Then they jumped back to the stump and popped into the hole for a rest.

After the tree-climbing lesson, Red's mother began to teach her babies about survival. She taught them what was good to eat: seeds, nuts, bark, buds, tree sap, and insects. She also showed them how to gather spruce cones and store them away for winter.

Life seemed perfect for the squirrel family—until the day Red got caught. Despite his mother's warnings, Red **ventured** onto the porch of the house that hunched at the edge of the woods. He'd spotted sunflower seeds there and couldn't resist an easy treat. Mr. Cooper spotted Red and came outside for a closer look. He frightened Red so badly that the little squirrel ran into a glass jar to hide. That was a mistake! Mr. Cooper's big hand went over the jar, and Red was caught.

Since Red was very young, Mr. Cooper probably thought he would become tame, but Red knew better. He was wild. He didn't want to be tamed. He ran around the cage Mr. Cooper put him in. He bit the metal bars and tried to **gnaw** his way out.

At first, when Mr. Cooper gave him nuts or bits of apple, Red snatched the food and tried to bite his hand. In time, however, Red grew used to Mr. Cooper. He began to take nuts from the man's hand. One day, when Red crept close to take a **tidbit,** Mr. Cooper picked him up and tried to pet him. Red struggled so hard to get away that he broke his tail. He fell to the floor and trembled.

"I'm so sorry, little Red," Mr. Cooper said, shaking his head. "I should have let you go that first day on the porch. With that broken tail, you'd better stay here through the winter so I can take care of you."

Mr. Cooper put Red back in the cage. He fed him and cared for him all winter. Red ate slices of juicy apples and nuts. He drank from a special water bottle. After he ate, Red did his exercises. He ran back and forth and climbed on the sides of the cage.

Sometimes he felt tame, and sometimes he felt wild. When he felt wild, he bit the cage and tried to escape. When he felt tame, he sat up and begged for food. But the tame feelings didn't last long. As soon as he finished his treat, all he could think of was getting back outside into the spruce forest.

The winter days passed slowly. Red's tail healed and became long and bushy. His reddish coat grew thick and shiny. Finally, the warm days came, and the snow melted. One sunny spring morning, Mr. Cooper set the cage outside on the porch and opened the little door. Quick as lightning, Red streaked out the door. He scampered up the nearest tree. He was free again!

Mr. Cooper smiled and waved from the porch as he watched Red hop from tree to tree, making his way deep into his forest home.

 **Comprehension Check**

1 Why does Red go onto Mr. Cooper's porch?

2 How does Red's life in the wild compare to his life in captivity?

3 Why do you think Mr. Cooper lets Red go free?

4 Do you think that people should try to capture and tame wild animals? Why or why not?

Vitamin L (for Lizard!)

by Rusty Fischer

Grover Mead found the lizard in his garage one morning. It looked sick and gray. He petted the lizard just like he would a dog and talked to him about things he thought a lizard might like to hear.

"What are you doing?" his older brother, Brad, asked when he found him in the garage.

"Look what I found," said Grover excitedly.

"A lizard? What's so special about that?" asked Brad as he headed off for a jog around the neighborhood. Grover figured he wouldn't be back for at least an hour.

"He doesn't know how cool you are," Grover told the lizard. "While Brad is out running, let's look in his room and see if we can find my missing comic books."

Grover carried the little lizard in the palm of his hand as he hurried into the house. He ignored the "KEEP OUT!" sign on his brother's door and snuck into Brad's room.

"Gross," Grover whispered as he stepped over a pile of dirty gym clothes. How could a health nut be such a slob? He dug through the mess, moving slowly from one side of the room to the other. Finally, beneath the table in the corner, he found his missing comics. As he put his hand on the table, he noticed all kinds of bottles and jars.

"Check these out," he said aloud. "These are Brad's super-duper ultra-vitamins. He claims they make him big and strong." There were B vitamins and E and A and D and a whole bunch of other letters, some with numbers, such as B_{12} and B_6. The

lizard lifted his head and **flicked** out his tongue.

"Hey!" Grover said out loud. "Maybe that's what you need! Vitamins!"

Grover carried his comics back to his room and looked in his dresser drawer for his hidden allowance. "Let's go down to the pet store and see if they have any vitamin L," he said. "For lizard!"

The pet store had just what he needed. After feeding the lizard some crickets dusted with vitamins, Grover poked holes in a shoebox and put the lizard inside. Then he stretched out on his lower bunk to rest.

Something loud pounded in Grover's head. A noise that sounded like growling! His sleepy eyes popped open and what he saw made him hope he was having a dream. His friendly little lizard had turned into a huge creature! The gigantic lizard took up almost the whole room. Its big, scaly head bent low to keep from popping right through the ceiling.

Grover rubbed his eyes, but the huge creature didn't turn back into a little gray lizard. He had never seen anything so big. Not even in the movies! He was just about to make a run for it when the lizard stretched out one huge claw and gently patted his knee. Then, if giant, scaly lizards could do such a thing, it smiled at him. "Thanks for the vitamins," said the lizard.

Wow! Grover thought. This is incredible. He thought about pinching himself to see if he was awake but decided against it. As long as his

gigantic lizard was friendly, why not just relax and enjoy it? As Grover smiled back at the lizard, the door to his room burst open.

"You were in my room while I was out, weren't you?" Brad **accused.** "What were you doing in there?"

Grover groaned. His brother didn't sound anything like a dream.

"Hey! I asked you a question," Brad shouted. "I expect an—"

A loud roar cut Grover's brother off. Brad looked up at the lizard, and the lizard looked back at Brad. This time the lizard didn't smile. Brad ran out of the room yelling.

"Thanks, buddy!" Grover said, reaching up to scratch the lizard beneath its scaly chin. If this was a dream, maybe he didn't want to wake up after all!

Comprehension Check

1 Why does Grover decide to feed vitamins to the lizard?

2 Based on clues from the story, what kind of person is Brad? How do you know?

3 Which parts of this story seem real and which seem like a dream?

4 Do you think Grover should keep the lizard he finds? Why or why not?

Where Was Her Mother?

by Vashanti Rahaman

Where was her mother? Keelo scrambled around the warm dark nest deep in the sand, listening to the roaring, rumbling sound. Around her, other baby green turtles scraped at the walls and ceiling of the nest too. Scraping and scrambling and trampling sand into the floor, they worked their way up to the surface and burst out of the nest onto the beach.

Where was her mother? Keelo did not want to stay on the beach. Though it was night, she sensed where the water was. Together, the babies scurried, tumbling down the beach past the crabs and birds and other creatures gathering to eat baby turtles with soft, new shells.

When Keelo made it to the sea, a wave reached out, lifted her off the sand, and wrapped her in wetness. Her flippers lost their clumsiness and moved easily now in graceful, flying strokes. Soon she was in deeper water, diving under the crashing waves, flying on water wings, out, out to sea.

Even here fish and birds waited to eat baby turtles, but Keelo escaped from them too. On and on she swam, away from the roaring, rumbling sound. Then the **current** caught her, like a river in the ocean. She swam with it for days. When she needed to rest, she folded her long front flippers back along her shell and slept, floating on the water.

At last the current left her in a place where the ocean was still and where mats of **sargassum weed** floated like rafts. Here baby turtles could hide, feed, and grow. But where was her mother? Could baby turtles grow up without mothers?

Keelo grew. When she was too big to hide in the seaweed, she swam away to **habitats** along the shore. But her mother was not there either. Where was her mother? Should Keelo even try to find her?

Keelo stayed near the shoreline. She ate sea grass and slept floating on the surface or on the sea bottom. She grew to be huge and strong. She had fewer enemies now, except for **harpoons,** fishing nets, and garbage that people put in the sea.

After many years, she set out toward the beach where she had hatched. For days she swam. Would she find her mother at last?

Finally, one day, she heard a familiar roaring, rumbling sound. She had come again to the beach of long ago. At first she stayed in the water with other big turtles. Then, one night, Keelo crept out of the sea.

In the darkness, the air felt dry. Without water to support her, Keelo felt **awkward.** She moved slowly. She stopped and looked around. She sensed that this was not yet the right spot.

Slowly, Keelo dragged herself up to a dry part of the beach. There she made a large **shallow** hole, and, at the bottom of the hole, she dug a tear-shaped pit. **Delicately,** she scooped up the sand with her **hind** flippers. She worked carefully, and though she had never done this before, she knew exactly what to do.

Keelo laid about 100 eggs. They were round and white like Ping-Pong® balls. Then she filled in the hole with sand and went back to the sea. She had answered nature's call; the eggs were as safe as she could make them, so she left them behind and swam away from the beach in the rumbling, crashing waves, returning to the shallow, calm waters where sea grass grew.

In Keelo's nest, deep in the sand, little green turtles grew inside her eggs. They would hatch soon and set out on their first great journey, crawling and then flying on water wings just as their mother had done. And just like her own mother, Keelo would not be there to see them.

Comprehension Check

1 What kind of turtle is Keelo?

2 At the beginning of the story, what does Keelo do when she cannot find her mother?

3 Why does Keelo come back to the beach where she was born?

4 Based on details from the story, what do you think might happen to Keelo's babies after they hatch?

Why So Brown, Isabelle?

by Shaunda Wenger

Isabelle flew around a misty, wet **marsh.** These **reeds** will provide a nice home, she thought. It's close to food and water, and there are plenty of grasses to hide my nest.

Isabelle gathered blades of brown, dried grass from a nearby hayfield and the surrounding marsh. Then she wove them among reeds that grew close together. She repeated this many times. By the fourth day, her work was done. The nest resembled a small basket. Isabelle went inside.

The next morning, Isabelle laid three pale blue, spotted eggs. Ferdinand stopped by for a visit.

"Isabelle, the eggs look great. Let me know when they hatch and I'll help take care of them."

Isabelle imagined their baby birds would look like Ferdinand. He was a proud red-winged blackbird. His bright red shoulder patches were edged with a thin, yellow stripe. They stood out against his black, shiny feathers. She admired Ferdinand when he perched on a **cattail** stalk, puffed out his colorful feathers, and sang his sweet song. "Konk-la-ree! Konk-la-ree!"

Many other brightly colored birds also caught Isabelle's eye. Whenever she left her nest to **forage** for insects or seeds, she commented on pretty **plumages** she saw along the way.

"Morning, Mr. Chickadee! Your black cap looks divine against your silver-gray feathers!

"Good afternoon, Mr. Swallow! Your steel-blue feathers sparkle brilliantly!

"Good evening, Mr. Oriole! Your orange plumage outshines the sun!"

Isabelle talked about other birds so much, it was amazing she found time to put food in her mouth.

One day Isabelle flew to a pool of clear water for a drink. She felt so tired from egg-sitting that she didn't look at anything around her. Instead, for the first time, she looked at her own reflection.

"Could it be? Is this me?" She looked closer. "Where are my red wing patches?" She looked longer. "Why am I brown with dark streaks? A red-winged blackbird can't be brown! What has happened to my beautiful plumage?" Away she flew, all in a flutter.

On her way home, she stopped and perched near some red **poppies.** It occurred to her that no one ever commented on how she looked. In fact, no one noticed her unless she called out first.

"Maybe I've been like this my whole life! Maybe I'll always be like this!" she worried.

She looked at the red poppies around her. They gave her an idea. She reached down, plucked some petals with her beak, and tucked them into her wings.

"There. That's better!" she exclaimed.

Isabelle stretched her neck and puffed out her feathers. She called out, "Konk-la-ree!" and away she flew.

When she got home, she settled into her nest. She waited for Ferdinand. What would he think?

Soon he flew into sight. Isabelle sat up tall, displaying her new wings. When Ferdinand saw her, he **veered** away and circled overhead.

"Check! Check! Tee-err!" he cried in warning. Suddenly he dove at Isabelle.

"Oh, no! Ferdinand, it's me! It's me, Isabelle!"

Ferdinand pulled out of his dive. He circled overhead again. Then he flew down and perched **cautiously** on the nest.

"What have you done to your feathers? I thought you were an **intruder!**" he exclaimed.

"I added color so I'd look like you. What do you think?" asked Isabelle.

"Well, you do look different. And now you can be seen in the nest. Do you think that's a good idea?"

"What do you mean?" she asked.

"Now everyone will notice you, including **predators.** It would be horrible if a raccoon or **mink** attacked our nest. You were **camouflaged** before."

"I didn't think of that." Isabelle shuddered. "I just wanted to look like a red-winged blackbird. I don't have red and yellow stripes on my wings, and I'm not black."

"Well, your brown color protects you from predators. It's hard to see you in these surroundings. Our young will be brown when they hatch for the same reason. The boys won't grow their colors until after the first year."

"I feel silly," said Isabelle. She plucked the red petals from her wings. "Why are you so colorful?"

"My colors helped get your attention." Ferdinand winked. "I knew you'd make a wonderful mother, so I competed with the other males to win your affection."

"Well, you certainly caught my eye."

"I'm lucky I did." Ferdinand puffed out his patches. "I'll be back in a flap with a nice insect snack." And off he flew.

Comprehension Check

1 What bird does Isabelle greet?

2 What does a male red-winged blackbird look like? A female?

3 Based on the information in the story, what do you think *camouflage* means?

4 What other colorful animals can you think of? What purpose do you think their colors serve?

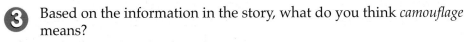

Mabel's Baby

by Diane E. Flader

Mabel drifted between the **mangrove** roots in the shallow, **brackish** waters of a Florida river. At the sounds of laughter, she **propelled** her 3,000-pound **bulk** with her paddlelike tail, nudging her infant along.

Cass and Drew squealed with delight when they recognized their gentle friends. "It's Mabel and her baby!" Cass announced to Drew. "They've come to visit us again."

Mabel swept up the infant and cradled him in her flippers, much like a human mother holding her child. She seemed to trust her human friends and feel comfortable near the riverbank behind their house. She pushed some water plants toward her baby's mouth with one flipper and watched him eat until he was satisfied.

"It's so cool the way she does that," said Drew. "You can tell that she really cares for her baby." He eyed the jagged scar above Mabel's right eye. "I hope she's able to keep him away from danger."

Cass wondered how long it would be before the infant manatee **encountered** a boat's propeller or a fisherman's net. The news was full of stories about the endangered manatees and their **perils** in the local waters.

Mabel cradled her infant, drifting back and forth for several minutes. Cass and Drew had plans to go fishing, but they watched silently in amazement until Mabel looked up at them as if to say good-bye for now.

"She is such a kind mother," Cass said dreamily as Mabel floated away.

"Well, we'd better go fishing before it gets too late," Drew reminded her.

They raced to the dock, where the boat was already loaded with fishing gear, and launched into the hot, **sultry** afternoon.

By the time they had been on the river for an hour, a dozen or more boats and jet skis had zoomed by them and stirred up the water. They retreated to their favorite fishing spot, called the Goldfish Bowl, where it was more private and quiet. They cast their lines and reeled them in with jerky motions to make their **lures** come alive and skip over the water.

"Come on. Bite!" urged an impatient Cass. "I want to have a fish fry tonight."

But Drew was confident. "Don't worry. We're going to catch one."

Then z-z-zing! Something big hit Cass's line. She set the hook and reeled in carefully. She would not let this one get away. Before long her prize surfaced beside the boat, shiny and silver, with a telltale dark stripe along its side. The **snook** thrashed about, trying in vain to free itself.

"I've got one!" she screamed.

"It's a snook, all right, but too small to keep," Drew said as he grabbed the net and snagged the fish. Carefully, he held it high for his sister to admire and removed the hook from its mouth. Then he tossed it back into the water and watched it swim quickly away.

Just then, they heard a **mournful** wail. It seemed as though the sound came from right under them.

"Did you hear that? It sounds like someone crying," whispered Cass. They both froze and then surveyed the water for any signs of distress. Then they heard it again.

Cass peered down into the water and saw Mabel peering back at her with big, sad eyes. Her baby was nowhere in sight. "It's Mabel! I think she's crying. Where is her baby?"

"I don't see him," Drew said. "Let's hope he's not far away." Drew recalled all of the boats and jet skis they had seen earlier; he hated to imagine what might have happened to Mabel's baby.

"Do you think she is trying to ask us to help her find him?" Cass asked. It certainly seemed that way to her. "I think we should go back toward home since that's the last place we saw them together. Mabel can follow us."

It was quiet on the water now, and the electric motor kept the boat moving at a pace slow enough for Mabel to follow. They cruised the edge of the river for what seemed like hours, but they had not even gone halfway home when they spotted a small fishing boat in the distance. They recognized the man aboard as their neighbor, Mr. Ives. When he saw them, he waved for them to approach.

"Hey there. Can you give me a hand?" he hollered.

"He must have landed something huge," Drew said. "Maybe a **tarpon**

or something." He waved back and answered, "Be right there."

Mabel snorted and rolled about. She swam away from the boat, and Cass was afraid they would lose her.

"I'll keep my eye on her," said Cass as Drew edged the boat close to the fisherman. The manatee's **stout** form would not be hard to locate now that they were in shallow water.

Mr. Ives pointed down into the water. "I remember seeing this baby manatee with its mother just last week," he said. "Can't be a year old yet, so he shouldn't be separated from her." The baby was behind the boat, fearful and grunting heavily. "I think the wake of those jet skis tore him loose from his mama and he got lost."

They turned to tell Mabel the good news, but she was already paddling to her baby's side.

The next morning Cass busily cut cardboard as Drew dipped a paintbrush into black paint. "I wonder if manatees get separated from each other every day," she said.

"I hope not, but one thing is for sure," said Drew. "I'm going to finish these signs as soon as I can and post them all over the river." Drew painted the final two letters of a sign that read "Slow Down! Manatee Crossing." Mabel and her baby were watching as he nailed the sign to the dock.

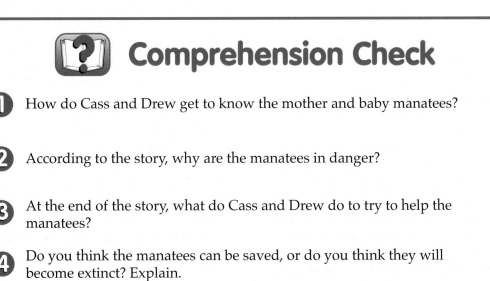

Comprehension Check

1. How do Cass and Drew get to know the mother and baby manatees?

2. According to the story, why are the manatees in danger?

3. At the end of the story, what do Cass and Drew do to try to help the manatees?

4. Do you think the manatees can be saved, or do you think they will become extinct? Explain.

Iitoi and the Butterflies

a Papago tale retold by Kim T. Griswell

Many, many seasons ago, Iitoi, the eldest son of Earth-Maker, wandered through the world. He drank in the sweet scent of growing things. He listened to the songs of the birds. He greeted the animals that poked their noses out to sniff the air as he passed by. He walked over mountains, across valleys, through streams, and into deserts. Everywhere he walked, he saw life, and his happy heart brought a smile to his face.

Then, one day, the air grew cold. The life around him began to die. When Iitoi walked in the woods, leaves fell from trees and crackled beneath his feet. He remembered how they had waved in the wind, green and alive as the rains washed over them. Now they lay brown and **lifeless**, waiting to return to the earth.

Iitoi sighed. Their beauty lasted for only a season. That was the way Earth-Maker said it must be.

As Iitoi walked, a few yellow leaves still clinging to a branch caught his eye.

"Before these too turn to dust," he said, "I will put them in my bag to keep their beauty alive." He gently plucked the leaves and placed them in his bag.

Iitoi walked on. He wandered into a field. Wildflowers bent their heads toward the ground. Their bright colors had faded. Soon they would return to the earth like the leaves.

Iitoi sighed. Their colors lasted for only a season. That was the way it must be.

As Iitoi walked, a few red, blue, and yellow flowers still standing tall caught his eye.

"Before these too fade away," he said, "I will put them in my bag to keep their colors bright." He picked the flowers and placed them in his bag.

Iitoi left the field and wandered into a village. Children circled him, laughing and calling his name. "Come and play with us, Iitoi," they said. "Our hearts are happy this day!"

Iitoi joined their game, but his heart grew heavy. If everything lasted only a season, these children too would grow old. They would spend their time warming themselves by the fires instead of playing. And one day they would return to the earth just as the leaves and the flowers.

Iitoi sighed. Childhood lasted only for a season. That was the way it must be. He wanted their happiness to stay with them when they grew old. He remembered the leaves and flowers he had placed in his bag. With those he could create something that would keep smiles on their faces even when they grew older.

He shook yellow **pollen** from a flower into the bag. He tossed in a handful of white cornmeal. He plucked green pine needles from the trees and stuffed those in as well. Then he opened the bag and let golden sunlight stream inside.

"What are you doing?" the children asked, dancing around Iitoi and his bag.

"Making something special for you," he replied. Then he picked up the bag, blew a breath into it, and shook it gently. When he opened the bag again, new and beautiful things flew out. Their wings were shaped like leaves. The colors of nature brightened their wings.

"I see blue and yellow wild-flowers flying!" said one child.

"I see green and red leaves dancing!" said another.

"What are these new creatures?" they asked.

"Butterflies!" said Iitoi, holding out his arm. Soon the butterflies **alighted** there. The children came closer. Their eyes widened. Their mouths opened in surprise. The butterflies shone like the sun and fluttered like leaves in the wind.

As Iitoi watched, the **elders** rose from their places by the fire and joined the children. Warm smiles spread across their faces. Happiness glittered in their eyes as Iitoi gently moved his arm and the butterflies filled the air once more.

Iitoi's butterflies dipped and soared around them. Like everything else, these butterflies would last only for a season. That was the way it must be. But they would return each year, bringing with them the colors of leaves and flowers, of pine and pollen, of cornmeal and sunshine. And each time they returned, the people would smile and their hearts would be happy.

Comprehension Check

1. What does Iitoi see when he wanders all over the world?

2. Why does Iitoi create butterflies?

3. Why do you think the Papago tell tales like this one?

4. If you could create a new creature, what would it look like?

The Landlord's Questions

an Irish folktale retold by Kim T. Griswell

There was never a sadder man in all of Ireland than Jack Murphy. His crops had failed. His cupboards were empty, and his wife had gone home to her mother. Then, one evening as the day turned to misty gray, the **landlord** knocked on Jack's door.

"Jack Murphy!" he called. "I've come for the rent."

Oh, Jack was in a sorry state. He had no money to pay the rent. He crept to the door with his head hanging nearly to his boots.

"Could you give me a bit more time, sir?" Jack asked.

Now the landlord had been eyeing Jack's farm for a long time. He'd much rather have Jack off the farm than collect the **meager** rent Jack owed him. He tapped a finger on his lips and tilted his head to one side.

"I'll tell you what," he said. "I'm feeling generous today, so I'll give you a bit of time."

Jack's face lit up in a great big grin.

"But, mind you, there's a catch," said the landlord with a wink.

Jack's face wrinkled into a frown. "And what kind of catch might there be?" he asked.

The landlord held up three fingers. "Three questions. If you can answer them all, you'll never have to pay rent again. You can farm this land until you rest your bones in the churchyard."

"And if I can't answer your questions?" asked Jack.

The landlord leaned forward and whispered, "Then you'll be off my land by sunrise, laddie. Deal?" He stuck out his hand.

Jack hesitated.

"Come now, Jack. Surely a clever lad like you can answer three simple questions!"

The **smug** look on his face told Jack that his landlord didn't think him very clever at all. But what could he do? Jack shook his landlord's hand.

"Now, then." The landlord rubbed his hands together. "Here are the three questions. First, how much does the moon weigh? Second, how many stars sparkle in the night sky? And third, what am I thinking?"

Oh, Jack was in a fine mess now. He'd be begging his mother-in-law for a place to sleep by sunrise.

"I'll be back first thing in the morning for your answers," said the landlord.

As the evening deepened into night, Jack put on his patched wool coat and went for a last walk over his farm. As he walked, Jack stared up at the moon. The narrow slice of moon only gave a fourth of its normal light.

"How much does the moon weigh?" he whispered to himself. "How much?" Then he snapped his fingers. "This lad's more

clever than his landlord thinks," said Jack.

His mood brightened a bit, and he tipped back his head to look at the stars.

"How many stars sparkle in the night sky?" He shook his head. "There are too many to count. I'm sure the landlord knows that very well. What am I to do?" He stared at the stars until they dazzled his eyes. Then he snapped his fingers. "This lad's more clever than his landlord thinks," said Jack.

Jack was sure he had the answers to the first two questions, but the third! How could he know what his landlord was thinking?

Jack nearly walked the soles off his boots. But when the sun warmed the green hillsides, he still did not know the answer to the third question. He headed home just in time to meet his landlord hurrying up the dusty lane.

"Well, my clever lad, are you ready to answer my questions?" The landlord's face already had a satisfied **flush**, as if he knew poor Jack would fail.

But Jack's own face brightened.

"I'm ready, sir," he said.

"All right, then. How much does the moon weigh?" he asked.

"Four quarters," said Jack.

The landlord's eyebrows raised. "And how many stars sparkle in the night sky?"

"All of them." Jack grinned.

The landlord's mouth dropped open. "And what am I thinking right now?"

"This lad's more clever than you thought!"

What could the landlord do? He nodded.

From that day on, there was never a happier fellow in all of Ireland than Jack Murphy. His crops grew like weeds. His wife returned home. And he lived on his farm rent-free until the day he rested his bones in the churchyard.

Comprehension Check

1. Why is Jack Murphy the saddest man in Ireland?

2. What three questions does Jack's landlord ask him?

3. Why do you think Jack says that the moon weighs four quarters?

4. What does Jack mean when he tells his landlord, "This lad's more clever than you thought"?

The Child Who Came From the Sea

an Irish folktale retold by Leanne Fanning Pankuch

In Ireland long ago, old Fisher Bran took his boat out on the sea. The day was fair. Fish jumped onto his hook. But, though his luck seemed good, Fisher Bran was unhappy. Each day he woke, dressed, ate breakfast, and fished. Each evening he stopped in the village to trade his catch for bread, buttermilk, and potatoes. Then he went home to his lonely cottage by the sea. Day followed day, the same sun rising and the same sun setting. Would it never end?

Then, one day, Fisher Bran felt a strong tug on his line. Using all of his strength to reel in the line, he hauled his catch up over the side of the boat.

"What manner of fish is this?" Fisher Bran exclaimed.

It wasn't a fish at all. It was a boy! Fisher Bran's hook was tangled in the boy's red hair.

"Well, we can't have that," the fisherman said. Gently, he removed the hook.

"What is your name, lad?" asked Fisher Bran.

The strange boy did not answer.

"I'll take you home with me," Fisher Bran decided.

The old fisherman stopped in the village. He traded his catch for a loaf of bread, a jug of buttermilk, and two potatoes.

"I caught this boy in the sea," he told the villagers proudly.

The villagers looked at each other and some shook their heads, but a young fisherman stepped forward and congratulated Fisher Bran. "What luck for you, sir," he said.

Fisher Bran's face shone with happiness. He said good night and took the boy home to his little house.

The old fisherman peeled and boiled the potatoes. He sliced the bread and poured two mugs of buttermilk. The boy was so hungry that he cleaned his plate. Fisher Bran smiled and the boy smiled back, but still, the boy said nothing.

In the morning, Fisher Bran began to teach the boy everything that he knew. He took the boy down to the beach and showed how the **sturdy** fishing boats were made by stretching **sailcloth** over **wicker** frames. The boy watched closely.

Later, they rowed the boat out to sea and began to fish. While they waited for their catch, Fisher Bran told stories of storms and whales and **ancient** sailors. At day's end, they returned to shore. The boy stood on the beach staring out toward the horizon.

"Come along," Fisher Bran said, pulling the boy away.

Each day Fisher Bran taught the boy something new. Soon the boy could tell when the weather was best for fishing. He could make strong fishing line and mend the boat when it became leaky, but something was not right.

Each night when Fisher Bran made him leave the sea, silent tears ran down the boy's face. One evening, he would not eat. The fisherman became worried. He took the boy to a wise woman in the village who was skilled in curing sickness. The wise woman listened to the old man's story. She looked into the boy's eyes.

"The cure is plain, but you won't like it," she said. "Take the boy out on the sea as near as you can to the spot where you caught him. Then you must throw him back."

"I can't do that!" Fisher Bran exclaimed. All he could think of was how lonely his life had been before he'd caught the boy.

Fisher Bran didn't sleep that night. He tossed and turned. He dreamed of waves crashing over his little home and a red-haired boy being swept out to sea with a great big smile on his face. When morning came, he knew what he must do.

He took the boy out on the sea as near as he could to the place where he had caught him.

"I want you to be well," he said. "But, I will miss you."

The boy hugged Fisher Bran before he ran to the bow of the boat and jumped high into the air. His laughter bubbled as he disappeared below the waves.

With tears on his wrinkled cheeks, Fisher Bran rowed for shore.

Back in the village, the wise woman had told the others what happened. Everyone felt sad for Fisher Bran. The youngest fisherman spoke up. "We all saw the fine job he did teaching that boy from the sea. Couldn't we send our own children to him to learn?"

What a grand idea! The villagers met Fisher Bran on the beach and asked if he would teach their children.

The old fisherman felt his heavy heart leap for joy!

"I will! I will!" he answered.

For many a year after that, Fisher Bran taught the village children the ways of the sea. He had a happy life. And, sometimes, as the old man turned his boat for home at day's end and **scanned** the horizon with his sharp eyes, he might see a red-haired boy lift his head above the water and smile.

Comprehension Check

1. Why is Fisher Bran unhappy at the beginning of the story?

2. What happens to change Fisher Bran's life?

3. Why do you think the wise woman tells Fisher Bran to take the child back to the sea?

4. How do you think teaching the village children will keep Fisher Bran from being unhappy again?

The Mayor's Solution

a fable retold by Kim T. Griswell

The women of the village of Nye were **content** with their everyday lives. Then one day a woman grumbled, "This village is **overrun** with mice!"

Another woman wrinkled her nose. "Mouse tracks in the flour barrel," she said.

"Holes gnawed in the walls!" said another.

"And a nest of newborns in my pillow!" said a third.

"We will go to the mayor and insist that he get rid of them at once."

So they pulled on their fall sweaters. They crunched down the leafy road and marched straight into the mayor's office.

"Good sir," said one woman, "we have a problem. Our homes are **swarming** with mice!"

"The solution is simple," said the mayor.

"Simple?" asked the woman.

The mayor nodded. "Cats! Cats are best for getting rid of these pests."

"Ah." The women nodded in admiration. "Cats."

So the mayor brought alley cats from all the neighboring villages. The mice fled into the fields beyond the village **boundaries**.

The women went contentedly back to their everyday lives. Then, one day, the same woman said, "This village is overrun with cats!"

Another woman sneezed. "Cat hairs on the furniture," she said.

"Claw marks on the floors!" said another.

"And a litter of kittens in my linens!" said a third.

"We will go to the mayor and insist that he get rid of them at once."

So they buttoned up their winter coats. They slipped down the icy road and marched straight into the mayor's office.

"Good sir," said one woman, "we have a problem. Our homes are crawling with cats!"

"The solution is simple," said the mayor.

"Simple?" asked the woman.

The mayor nodded. "Dogs! Dogs are best for getting rid of these pests."

"Ah." The women nodded in admiration. "Dogs."

So the mayor brought stray dogs from all the neighboring villages. The cats fled into the hills beyond the village boundaries.

The women went contentedly back to their everyday lives. Then, one day, the same woman said, "This village is overrun with dogs!"

Another woman scratched her legs. "Fleas in the bedclothes," she said.

"Pawprints on the rugs!" said another.

"And a **passel** of puppies in my pajamas!" said a third.

"We will go to the mayor and insist that he get rid of them at once."

So they zipped up their spring dresses. They hurried down the muddy road and marched straight into the mayor's office.

"Good sir," said one woman, "we have a problem. Our homes are drowning in dogs!"

"The solution is simple," said the mayor.

"Simple?" asked the woman.

The mayor nodded. "Bulls! Bulls are best for getting rid of these pests."

"Ah." The women nodded in admiration. "Bulls."

So the mayor brought big bulls from all the neighboring villages. The dogs fled into the forest beyond the village boundaries.

The women went contentedly back to their everyday lives. Then, one day, the same woman said, "This village is overrun with bulls!"

Another woman straightened her skirt. "Hoofprints in the front yard," she said.

"China crushed all over the kitchen!" said another.

"And calves in my cabinet!" said a third.

"We will go to the mayor and insist that he get rid of them at once."

So they opened their **parasols** to shield them from the hot sun. They slowly walked down the dusty road and marched straight into the mayor's office.

"Good sir," said one woman, "we have a problem. Our homes are bursting with bulls!"

"The solution is simple," said the mayor.

"Simple?" asked the woman.

The mayor nodded. "Elephants! Elephants are best for getting rid of these pests."

"Ah." The women nodded in admiration. "Elephants."

So the mayor brought trumpeting elephants from all the neighboring villages. The bulls fled into the pastures beyond the village boundaries.

The women went contentedly back to their everyday lives. Then, one day, the same woman said, "This village is overrun with elephants!"

Another woman wiped her brow. "Peanut shells in the soup," she said.

"**Craters** stomped in the garden!" said another.

"And a baby elephant bathing in my bathtub!" said a third.

"We will go to the mayor and insist that he get rid of them at once."

So they pulled on their fall sweaters. They crunched down the leafy road and marched straight into the mayor's office.

"Good sir," said one woman, "we have a problem. Our homes are infested with elephants!"

"The solution is simple," said the mayor.

"Simple?" asked the woman.

The mayor nodded. "Mice! Mice are best for getting rid of these pests."

"Ah." The women nodded in admiration. "Mice."

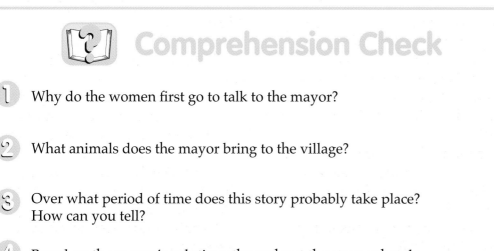

Comprehension Check

1. Why do the women first go to talk to the mayor?

2. What animals does the mayor bring to the village?

3. Over what period of time does this story probably take place? How can you tell?

4. Based on the mayor's solutions throughout the story, what do you think will happen when the mice come back to the village?

Three Fears of the Dragon

by Kim T. Griswell

Po Sing watched his mother paint the door of their house bright red.

"Mother, why do we paint the door for the new year?" he asked.

"Because of Nian," she said, smiling.

"Nian?"

"Yes." She put down her brush, sat down on the couch near the crackling fire, and patted the seat beside her. Po Sing sat. "Nian was an ugly, **ferocious** dragon that lived long ago." This is his story.

Every year as the days grew shorter, colder, and darker, the villagers hid behind the doors of their mud houses; their bones shook in their skin as they waited for Nian to come. The five-toed dragon was a monster unlike any other. He had the eyes of a rabbit, the antlers of a deer, the whiskers of a catfish, the body of a **serpent**, and the **talons** of an eagle. When his belly rumbled with hunger, he came down from the mountains to find a meal.

"What are we to do?" one old woman asked. Her **withered** hands clutched and unclutched in her lap and she could not still them.

"We cannot fight him," said one man.

"He will kill us all!" moaned another.

The wisest man in the village was very old. Throughout his life, when Nian raged through the village, he had not hidden behind barred doors; he had watched and learned. He cleared his throat and peered through aging eyes at the villagers crouched around the hut.

"Every creature fears something," he said. "You fear Nian. But what does Nian fear?"

A young man bowed toward the elder. "Father, had I the teeth and claws of Nian, what should I fear?"

The ancient man's wrinkled lips thinned into a smile. "For many years I have watched the monster, and I know his fears. I have cast the oracle bones. They tell that Nian will come tomorrow night. If you follow my guidance, I believe we can rid ourselves of the monster forever."

All through the day, the old man guided the women as they stitched together red cloth into long, flowing banners. When the sun faded behind the mountain and Nian roared forth, they stood outside their huts for the first time in years. Each villager held a banner in fear-tightened hands.

"You must wait until he is almost upon you," the old man said.

As Nian entered the village, he tossed his antlers; his huge eyes gleamed red as he **bared** his teeth. A few villagers dropped their banners and fled, but many stood their ground. The old man lifted his banner, and the remaining villagers followed his lead, waving their banners in the air.

Nian stopped his charge. His rabbit eyes widened. His catfish whiskers twitched. His serpent body **writhed** and his talons tore clods from the dirt. Then he turned and fled.

"We have done it!" the villagers cheered. "Nian is defeated."

But when the old man cast the oracle bones, he shook his head. "The dragon will return tomorrow. We must work quickly to prepare."

The old man instructed them to build a huge bonfire. They piled paper, sticks, and thick branches in the center of the village. Darkness fell cold and starless. The villagers held their banners once more, while the old man stood alone beside the bonfire. When Nian's roar filled the sky, he lit a torch.

Nian sprang into the village, clawing at the first mud huts he came to. The villagers flapped their banners in the wind. The old man touched the torch to the paper at the base of the bonfire. It smoked and sputtered, but soon fire licked the branches and gobbled them with its blazing tongue. Nian reared back on his **haunches**, roaring in fear.

Above the fire's answering roar, the old man shouted, "Flee from here, Nian, and we will let you live!"

When Nian fled, the villagers sang and danced around the bonfire. The old man crept into his hut to cast the oracle bones again.

"Father! Your plan has worked!" His smiling son peered into the smoky hut, but the old man shook his head.

"Tomorrow night, Nian will return," he said. "We must prepare one last surprise."

The next day, the villagers built a new bonfire. They unfurled their red banners. When Nian roared into the village, they were ready.

Banners waved, the bonfire raged, but this time, the dragon did not flee. His sharp, rabbit eyes sought out the old man standing near the bonfire. He clawed through the villagers, clasped the old man in his eaglelike talons, and opened his great jaws.

"Now!" the old man shouted.

As one, the villagers tossed their bamboo tubes into the fire. The tubes blackened, smoldered, and hissed. Then they began to explode. Blam! Wham! The air filled with such a great noise that Nian released the old man and sprang back. Tube after tube burst. The air filled with **billowy** smoke and blazing flashes. Nian fled.

"And this time, he never returned," Po Sing's mother said, returning him to the present.

"So the red door is like the banners the villagers waved," he said.

His mother nodded as she rose and picked up her brush to **resume** her careful painting. Tonight, Po Sing would throw a flashing string of firecrackers out the front door at the stroke of midnight. Now he knew why. Nian was afraid of three things: the color red, blazing fires, and noise. Tonight, Po Sing would help keep Nian away.

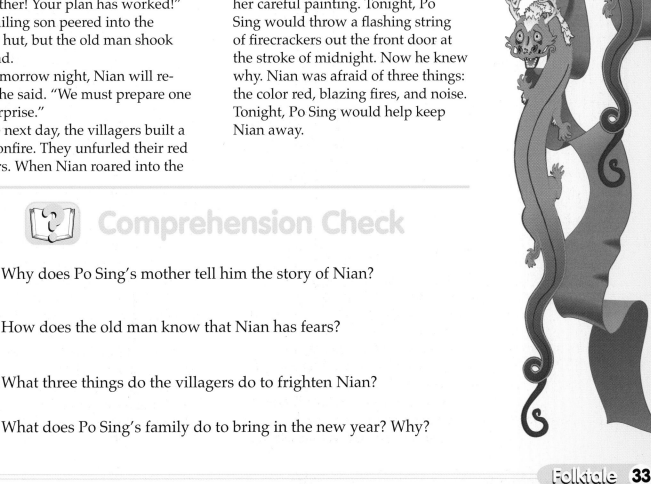

Comprehension Check

1. Why does Po Sing's mother tell him the story of Nian?

2. How does the old man know that Nian has fears?

3. What three things do the villagers do to frighten Nian?

4. What does Po Sing's family do to bring in the new year? Why?

Freedom School

by Beverly J. Letchworth

Lithia Ann shivered in the gray October dawn of 1851. Her thin green **shawl** could not keep out the cold wind blowing in **gusts** off the water. Her friend, Mattie, and three other children waited on the riverbank with her.

Lithia Ann patted the sack she carried. She could feel the apple and the soft bulge of corn bread inside. They would be her lunch. Her apron fabric was rolled in the bottom of the bag. But she could feel no **thimble.** Had she forgotten to bring it? What about the needle?

Crouching, she pulled everything out of her bag. She searched the material for the needle, but could find neither it nor the thimble. She had left them at home!

Mattie stooped beside her. "What's wrong?"

"I forgot my needle and thimble. What if they come and see that I don't have them?"

"Nobody's come for a long time," Mattie said, looking toward the water. "Reverend Meachum's almost here. Come on."

Lithia Ann stuffed her belongings back into the sack and watched the flat-bottomed boat glide closer. Reverend Meachum pulled strongly on the oars. The boat scraped the riverbank and stopped. Lithia Ann, Mattie, and the other children scrambled into the boat.

Reverend Meachum turned the **skiff** and headed out into the Mississippi River. "Ready for another day of learning?" he asked the children brightly. "You know education is the key to our success as free people."

"Yes, Reverend Meachum," the children replied together.

Lithia Ann glanced at Mattie, who winked. Every day he said the same thing, yet Lithia Ann knew how important his words were. After all, Reverend Meachum had once been a slave. But he had become educated, bought his freedom, and was now a successful Missouri businessperson and minister. Lithia Ann wanted nothing less for herself.

Within a few minutes, they neared the steamboat anchored in the middle of the river. The children climbed aboard, waving to Mr. Jake in the pilothouse. He was their lookout. He would warn them if anyone came. Hurrying to their benches, they murmured hellos to the others. Miss Wolen, the teacher, held up her hand for silence.

Lithia Ann **wedged** her sack against her thigh. It seemed to burn through her dress, so aware was she that she hadn't brought the needle and thimble. But there was nothing to do about it now. She would just have to pretend she was sewing if the authorities came and questioned them about what they were doing on the boat. Like before, they would tell them that they were learning to sew. Couldn't they see all the fabric and needles and thread? And the boys were learning carpentry. Surely they could see the wood and hammers and nails.

What the authorities wouldn't see were the books quickly hidden away when the warning came. What they wouldn't know was that school was in session in this steamboat in the middle of the river, and that the children were learning to read and write.

Like Reverend Meachum said, "Our people have the right to be educated, even though the law says otherwise."

Miss Wolen handed out the books. "Lithia Ann, will you read from page 19?"

Lithia Ann turned to the correct page, stood up, and began to read. She finished the paragraph and sat back down, her face warm with pride. She knew she was still slow, but she'd get better. Already she could read signs and the names of stores. Soon she'd be able to read and write everything she wanted.

Lithia Ann glanced at the other kids around her. None of them would ever forget Reverend Meachum's freedom school, she thought, and no one could take away the education they gained here.

 Comprehension Check

1. What is Lithia Ann concerned about at the beginning of the story?

2. If the authorities come aboard and ask what the children are doing, what will they tell them?

3. Why are the children going to the steamboat in the middle of the river?

4. Why do the children have to hide the fact that they are learning to read and write?

A Tin Cup Full

by Jennifer Riesmeyer Elvgren

Anna stood on a bench in the front hall, saluting herself in the mirror.

"You can't be a soldier," laughed her oldest sister Sadie from the parlor.

"They don't allow girls," chimed in her middle sister Lucy.

"I want to be ready just in case." Anna jumped to the floor and peered out the door, watching for the soldiers.

For most of the afternoon, cannons and shells had boomed in the distance as the Confederate and Union troops began to fight on the hills surrounding the girls' Gettysburg farm.

"Don't go outside, Anna. It's not safe," Papa yelled from his study. "Besides, there's much work to be done for our Union boys before dark."

Anna hurried to the kitchen where Mama bent over a table, furiously **kneading** another ball of bread dough.

"Our troops must be half-starved." She wiped some flour from her cheek, frowning when she heard cannon fire.

"I'll stir this one," said Anna, kneeling on a chair and using a large wooden spoon to mix the flour, water, yeast, salt, sugar, and oil. As the ingredients swirled round and round in the old yellow bowl, Anna wondered how loud it would be if she were standing next to a thundering cannon.

"Kaboom!" she screamed.

"Ahhhhh!" Mama screeched and jumped a foot in the air. The dough slipped out of her hands and landed on the floor.

"I'm sorry, Mama," Anna cried.

"Out! Out! Out of this kitchen at once!" Mama stomped her foot, pointing to the door.

Anna wandered into the parlor where Lucy and Sadie sat on the floor surrounded by fresh flowers, lace, and ribbon. Usually full of giggles, the girls sat in silence, their fingers flying as they tied ribbons around flower bouquets.

"What are you making?" Anna said as she picked up some red ribbon.

"Bouquets for the soldiers," replied Sadie. "When they march by into battle, we'll give them one to cheer them."

"I'll help." Anna began gathering daisies. As she arranged the flowers, she wondered what it would be like to march all day.

"Left. Right. Left. Right. Left. Right." Anna marched over several finished bouquets, squashing them.

"They're ruined!" wailed Lucy.

"I didn't see them," Anna moaned.

"Get away from the flowers! Go bother Papa. Now!" snapped Sadie.

Papa poked his head out of the study door.

"Anna, come help me make bandages," he called. "I'm going to need quite a few when I ride into town to help treat the wounded."

Anna brushed flower petals from her skirt and followed Papa into the study. Using all the **muslin** that they owned, Papa tore the cloth into long strips.

"Make sure that they're wide too," he instructed. Papa flinched as gunshots cracked through the air.

While ripping the muslin, Anna wondered if she could escape the shooters. Pretending she was dodging bullets, Anna bumped Papa's medicine cabinet, knocking over his medicine bottles. Papa's medical books were soaked.

"To your room, Anna!" Papa shouted.

Anna fought back tears as she walked up the stairs. "I just wanted to help," she whispered as she flopped onto her bed.

Rat a tat tat. Rat a tat tat. Tat. Tat. Rat a tat tat. The beating of a drum sent Anna scurrying to the window where she saw a Union reserve unit marching toward the battle, led by a drummer boy.

"He looks awfully hot—tired too," Anna thought out loud. She wondered what it would be like to walk for days in the heat.

Water, she thought. He needs some water. She dashed down the stairs and out the door, racing toward the **springhouse.**

Anna filled a large tin cup with cold spring water and offered it to the drummer boy. He drained the cup as he marched.

"Thank you, miss. We've marched at least 20 miles today." He wiped his mouth with the back of his hand.

With water sloshing over the brim of the cup, Anna sprinted back and forth until he had drunk his fill.

"Godspeed!" She waved to him and the other soldiers from the roadside.

An officer pulled up his horse in front of Anna.

"Thank you for giving the drummer water. He helps us all to keep marching." He smiled. "What's your name?"

"Anna." She squinted, looking up at him.

"I'm General Meade. Pleased to meet you." He winked. "I think you'd make a fine soldier."

"Papa! Mama! Lucy! Come quick—it's Anna!" Sadie shouted from the **parlor** window. Anna's family gathered on the porch as General Meade stood in his **stirrups** and saluted her.

Beaming, Anna stood tall and saluted General Meade back, as Mama, Papa, Sadie, and Lucy handed out bread and bouquets to the soldiers.

Comprehension Check

1 Based on facts given in the story, what war is being fought when this story takes place?

2 What does Anna dream of doing? Why do you think she would want to do that?

3 What always seems to happen when Anna tries to help? Why?

4 How does Anna finally offer to help the soldiers?

The Daring Doodler of Marceline, Missouri

by Kim T. Griswell

"Come on, Grandpa!" Arnie shouted as he hopped off the chunky red-and-yellow Jolly Trolley. They'd ridden it from one end of Toontown to the other. Arnie was trying to talk his grandpa into getting in line to ride Gadget's Go Coaster when someone tapped him on the shoulder.

"I bet Walter Elias's parents had no idea they were in some way responsible for bringing a mouse, a duck, a cricket, and a very goofy pup into the world when he was born," said a strange voice.

Arnie turned around, expecting to see a guy who liked to **gab** as much as his grandpa. Instead he faced a giant mouse wearing huge black shoes, red pants with fat white buttons, and a bright yellow bow tie. "Who is Walter Elias?" Arnie asked.

The giant mouse put a hand on the side of his face. "You've never heard of Walter Elias? The daring doodler of Marceline, Missouri?"

Arnie shook his head.

"Well!" the mouse said, taking Arnie's hand. "Walk with me for a while, and I'll give you the scoop."

Arnie gave his grandpa a questioning look. "Go ahead. I could use a rest," his grandpa said as he wandered toward a shaded bench.

As they headed away from the coaster, the mouse started talking.

"Walter Elias spent most of his childhood on a farm in Marceline, Missouri. He was an **imaginative** boy, a dreamer. The kind of kid who doodled in class instead of doing his schoolwork."

"I like to doodle," said Arnie.

The mouse nodded. "Lots of kids like to doodle, but few of them know that doodles can lead to big things!"

"Like what?" Arnie said with a frown.

"Hang on," said the mouse. "We'll get to that soon enough."

They wandered past Space Mountain. Arnie would have asked the mouse to get on the ride with him, but he didn't think those giant black shoes would fit in a roller coaster car.

"Some of Walter's teachers let him tell stories to his classmates and **illustrate** them on the chalkboard," continued the mouse.

"I wish my teachers would let me do that," Arnie said.

"As might be expected," the mouse went on, "Walter Elias became one of those guys who never wanted to grow up. He didn't see much sense in working hard if he couldn't keep the feeling of happy excitement he had as a kid."

"You mean the kind of feeling you get when you come to an amusement park like this one?" asked Arnie. They had just passed a ride with giant teacups. Arnie could hardly wait to spin himself silly in one of those cups.

The mouse nodded. "Exactly. Walter Elias decided to start a cartoon company with his big brother Roy. Before long, they had their first cartoon order and then they had to **expand** their business!

"One day he was doodling on his drawing pad as he rode on a train. Before long, the doodle turned into a mouse. Later in life, Walter told everyone that his success all started with a mouse.

"Walter made his mouse the star of a cartoon called *Steamboat Willie.* The mouse danced across the screen in black and white as music played in the background."

"Black and white?" asked Arnie.

The mouse bent low and whispered in Arnie's ear, "The first animated cartoons weren't in color."

"What?" Arnie couldn't believe that.

"It's true," the mouse said, patting him on the shoulder. "Later Walter Elias added color to his cartoons. For two years, he held the **patent** on a process called Technicolor. That made him the only person who could make color cartoons."

"I wonder if I've ever seen any of them," Arnie said.

"I bet you have," the mouse said. They'd circled the park and now stood in the entrance, right in front of the Main Street Railroad Station.

"Despite all the hard work Walter did to make his cartoons, he still had plenty of imagination left over," the mouse continued. "So in 1955, he turned a **grove** of orange and walnut trees into a magical kingdom. His kingdom had mountains, rivers, and castles. Everybody he talked to said

his magical place would be a flop, but Walter was a daring kind of guy. He used all the money he could pull together to build his kingdom.

"Fortunately for Walter, people loved his magical kingdom. His **daring** risk became a big success."

The mouse put his white-gloved hands on his hips and frowned.

"I wonder if the teachers who tried to keep Walter Elias from doodling knew that he earned more than 30 Academy Awards?"

"Academy Awards?" Arnie stared. "What films did this Walter Elias guy make, anyway?"

"Well, let me see." The mouse tapped the side of his face. *"Snow White and the Seven Dwarfs, Pinocchio,* and *Fantasia* were some of his best," he said.

"Wait a minute!" Arnie spun around. "Are you telling me that Walter Elias was Walter Elias *Disney?* Walt Disney? The guy who created this park?"

"Yes, he was." The mouse beamed.

"Disneyland," Arnie whispered. "That makes Walter Elias the guy who created Donald Duck and Jiminy Cricket and Goofy! And—"

"And me." Arnie's companion bowed. "Mickey Mouse, at your service."

❓ Comprehension Check

1. What kind of a child was Walt Disney?

2. Besides cartoons, what else did Walt Disney create?

3. This story begins by saying that Walter Elias's parents were partly responsible for bringing into the world a mouse, a duck, a cricket, and a goofy pup when their son was born. To which famous cartoon characters does this statement refer?

4. Which of Walt Disney's creations do you most enjoy? Why?

Riding the Switchback

by Kim T. Griswell

Joseph followed his best friend, Hiram, up the dirt road toward the Mauch Chunk mine.

"How much farther?" he asked.

"It's getting steeper," Hiram replied, "so we must be near the top."

"Good," Joseph said.

Both of their fathers worked for Mr. Josiah White, the businessman who owned the mines in Summit Hill. Hiram's father dug coal, and Joseph's pa was the **brakeman** on the Switchback Gravity Railroad, built in 1827. He operated the brake lever as trains loaded with coal sped down the hill. He came home each night with his arms aching and his muscles bulging. Joseph figured it took a lot of courage to ride the Switchback. It traveled nine miles downhill from the mine to the river landing in Mauch Chunk. It could reach speeds of 100 miles per hour.

When Hiram suggested that they sneak up the hill after dark and take a ride on the Switchback, Joseph tried every excuse he could think of to avoid going.

"Guess your pa got all the nerve in your family," Hiram teased.

Joseph didn't want his best friend to think he was chicken, so he followed Hiram up the mountain in the dead of night. Finally, they reached the **summit.**

"There it is!" Hiram shouted as he lifted the lantern high. "The ride of the century!"

A chunky metal **railcar** waited at the top of the **incline,** ready to be loaded with coal the next day. Hiram set the lantern inside and looked at Joseph. Both boys had watched the miners often enough to know how to start the car rolling. The Switchback had the highest **inclined plane** of any railroad of its time. All you had to do was give the car a shove, and **gravity** did the rest.

"I'll push off, if you'll work the brake," Hiram offered.

Joseph jumped into the cart. His hands felt **gritty** as he grabbed the brake lever. His throat felt tight. It felt as if he sat on the edge of the world.

Hiram pushed with all his strength. Then he climbed aboard the car before it could pick up speed.

"Keep it steady," he said.

Joseph clutched the brake. The first section of track terrified him. It was a wooden **span** of railroad **ties** and rails. If he lost control of the car, it would plunge down, down, down!

By the light of the lantern, he could tell when they made it across the **trestle,** but that was only the first small section. Soon, they were switching back and forth, around the curve of a mountain, across a gushing stream, past trees. The muscles in Joseph's arms began to burn as he pumped the brake to keep their speed low.

In the back of the car, Hiram shouted with glee. Joseph felt too much responsibility for their safety to enjoy it too much.

His arms began to shake because he was so tired. Just then, the ground leveled out. He could see the lights of the river landing up ahead. One last time, he grasped the brake and then pulled with all the strength he had left. The brakes screeched. Sparks flew up on both sides of the car. At last, they rolled to a stop.

Hiram thumped him on the back. "Wasn't that the greatest ride of your life?" he asked.

Now that he could let go of the brake, Joseph started to grin. "Yeah! It nearly scared me to death!"

"Trouble," Hiram whispered, looking over Joseph's shoulder.

Joseph turned. Standing on the platform staring at them was Mr. Josiah White, the mine's owner.

"What do you two boys think you are doing?" he asked.

"I'm sorry, Mr. White," Joseph apologized. "We just wanted to take a ride on the Switchback."

Mr. White seemed to think for a minute. "Do you think others would want to take such a ride?" he asked.

Both Hiram and Joseph nodded enthusiastically.

"I think you've hit on something, boys!" Mr. White said. "Why should my train sit **idle** in the evenings when I could make some money? Now, let me think, what might people pay?"

He looked at Joseph and asked, "Young man, what would you pay for a ride on the Switchback?"

"Fifty cents?" Joseph suggested.

"Fifty cents it is!" Mr. White announced. "A real bargain, if I say so myself! And you two can earn the 50 cents you owe me by riding a couple of mules down the mountain and hauling this car back up."

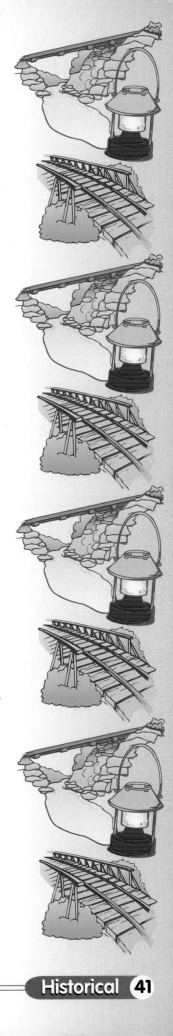

❓ Comprehension Check

1 Where and when does this story take place?

2 What kind of work do Joseph's and Hiram's fathers do?

3 Although the characters in this story are fictitious, the Switchback Gravity Railroad is not. What common amusement park ride do you think it led to?

4 If you could take something ordinary and turn it into an amusement park ride, what would you choose? Why?

A Boy Like Me

by Kim T. Griswell

Nine-year-old Samuel streaked ahead of his best friend, John, as they raced toward the wooden rail fence. The mountains rose blue and misty just beyond the pines. On this early summer morning in 1838, the air curling through the north Georgia valley smelled of honeysuckle and wood smoke. Samuel filled his lungs with the sweet air and **surged** forward.

"I won!" he called, touching the fence post.

As he turned, he noticed that John had stopped a few feet away. He stood as still as a statue and frowned as he gazed across the field.

"Is my father coming?" Samuel asked, hurrying toward his friend.

John shook his head. "Strangers," he said, pointing.

Samuel shielded his eyes. A group of uniformed men on horseback rode up the dirt drive toward his **sturdy** log home. A shock of fear went through Samuel when one man stomped up the porch steps and kicked open the front door. The others followed him closely.

"Come on," Samuel whispered.

The boys crept onto the back **stoop** and peered through a window.

"What are they doing?" John asked.

As they watched, one of the men knocked a pottery bowl from the kitchen table. It shattered in a rain of red powder. Another man pulled open a drawer of the **sideboard** and began **rifling** through its contents. Samuel's mother stood silently, her hands twisting her apron like a rope.

The man who had kicked open the door stepped forward.

"We're here on General Scott's orders to remove you from these **premises,**" he said.

Samuel's mother clutched at the chair behind her.

"You can't do that!" she said. "This is our home. These lands belong to the Ani´-Yun´wiya, the Cherokees."

"Your people," he replied, "signed a **treaty** agreeing to leave. You've got to go!" His eyes were as cold as glass.

"I've got to warn my family," John said.

As John fled toward the woods behind the house, Samuel headed toward the front yard. His legs moved slowly. When he turned the corner of the house, he clenched his fists. His mother stood staring at the house, as if looking at it for the last time. In her hands, she clutched a few blankets. A black **shawl** drooped from one sagging shoulder. Samuel wanted to rush at the men, to order them to leave, but what could he do against these soldiers? He was just a boy.

The man who had spoken to Samuel's mother pointed to two of his men. They mounted their horses and headed across the pasture. Samuel's father and uncle were just beyond the trees, hoeing mounds of dirt around the new plants in their garden. He hoped that the soldiers would not find them. A few minutes later, the men returned, herding his father and uncle before them.

Samuel's heart began to burn. Who were these men to drive them from their home? His people had lived on this land long before the white men came. Samuel saw the anger in his father's eyes. What would his father do? What could he do? Nothing, Samuel realized. Nothing but go where the men led them.

When they reached their **destination,** Samuel looked up at his mother. She squeezed his hand reassuringly. They passed through the gates of a small **stockade.** The soldiers pushed them into this pen that looked like it had been built for animals. Samuel felt tears forming in his eyes, but he refused to cry in front of his captors.

Each night in the pen, he huddled close to his parents for warmth. His belly rumbled with hunger. Day blurred into day. Months passed. Summer swam into fall. The air grew colder. The ground froze each night, forcing them to sleep on a mattress of ice. The image of that last spring day of **carefree** play faded from Samuel's mind. Then, one day, the soldiers opened the gates.

Were they to be freed at last? Samuel took his mother's hand and walked slowly along with the others, but they were not walking toward freedom. Before their long walk ended, a hundred days would pass. The Cherokee families who had been taken from their homes would walk all the way to Oklahoma. About 4,000 people would die along the way. The Cherokee people called this cruel march *nuna dat shun´yi,* the "trail where they cried."

As they passed towns, people lined the roads to watch. They said nothing. Samuel wanted to shout at them.

"How dare you stand there with your full bellies, dressed in your warm woolen clothes, and do nothing!"

Samuel caught the eye of a white boy about his age. He wondered what the boy saw when he looked at him. Did he see another boy? Someone who could have been a friend? Someone who could swim, race, and play?

One of the boy's fists was clenched in front of him. He sees only the color of my skin, Samuel decided. He sees the color of the red clay he stands on. And I see his skin—white, the color of milk.

But as Samuel passed, the boy opened his fist and reached his palm toward him. In it, he held a crab apple. Samuel looked up in surprise.

"You can have it, if you want," the boy said. He smiled.

Samuel reached for the fruit, but he could not return the boy's smile. He wondered if he would ever smile again. Maybe someday he would, when everyone learned to see what this boy could see. Boys are just boys, no matter what color their skin. Boys like him, he nodded to the boy as he bit into the apple, boys like me.

Comprehension Check

1 What happens to change Samuel's life at the beginning of the story?

2 Why do the soldiers say that Samuel's family must leave its home?

3 Why do you think the Cherokees called this time in history the "trail where they cried"?

4 Do you think that people today see one another without regard to skin color? Why or why not?

Third-Grade Daredevil

by Natasha Wing

Albert was the kind of kid who got overlooked a lot. He was quiet and small, and not many of the kids in his class seemed to know he existed. He wished they did, but how could he get them to?

One afternoon, as Albert watched television, **daredevil** Robbie Knievel revved up his motorcycle for his big jump across the Grand Canyon. Cameras flashed. Fireworks erupted. People cheered. Everyone wanted his autograph.

If I were a daredevil, people would notice me, Albert thought.

He got on his bike and jumped over sidewalk cracks, puddles, and sticks. After weeks of practicing, Albert was ready to do a big jump in front of an audience. When he got to school, he hung a poster on the wall.

It read, "Come see Albert jump 20 phone books with his bike! Friday after school in the school parking lot."

After his teacher, Miss Cruz, saw the poster, she called him up to her desk.

Albert straightened his shoulders and tried to look tall as he walked up to her desk. His plan was working. He was already getting attention from his teacher. Maybe she wanted his autograph!

"How are you going to jump those phone books?" Miss Cruz asked.

"With my bike," said Albert.

"Do you have a helmet?"

Albert frowned. "No," he said.

"Knee or elbow pads?"

"No." His shoulders slumped, and he shook his head.

"Then I can't allow you to jump at school," said Miss Cruz. "It wouldn't be safe."

Albert's heart sank. If he had to give up his plan to become a daredevil, he'd never get noticed.

"Please, Miss Cruz," he begged. "I've been practicing, and I'm almost as good as Robbie Knievel."

Miss Cruz looked at Albert long and hard. He straightened up again, trying to look taller.

"Okay," she said at last, "but I'm sure Robbie Knievel jumped smaller things before he jumped the Grand Canyon. You can jump using your feet only. And I want you to jump something that's safe."

Safe! What good was it to jump something safe? He'd never get noticed doing that. Besides, he had practiced jumping with his bike, not his feet. He wondered what Robbie Knievel would do. He wouldn't give up, that's what. If Albert couldn't jump the Grand Canyon, he would try to jump something else.

"Do you have 20 chalkboard erasers?" he asked.

"I could get them," said Miss Cruz.

"Then that's what I'll jump."

At recess Albert inspected the sand pit. Josh, the math whiz, wandered over.

"Do you know how many feet 20 erasers equal?" Josh asked.

"Four?" guessed Albert.

"Try about eight," said Josh. "That's twice your height. You can't jump eight feet."

"Can too," said Albert. He **tensed** his legs and jumped into the sand.

"That's about four feet," said Josh.

"I'm just warming up," said Albert, but he was worried. Was four feet all he could clear? If only he had his bike! He could clear eight feet easily with it.

By the end of recess, Albert had jumped about five feet.

Albert practiced some more after school.

On Friday morning, he woke up with sore legs and a knot in his stomach. Josh's words rang in his ears, "You can't jump eight feet."

He went to school without eating.

"Big day today, Albert," said kids in the hallway.

All during silent reading, Albert worried that he'd land short of his goal in front of his classmates. Twenty erasers are a lot, he thought. Why didn't I say I could jump ten?

When he went to art class, the art teacher lent Albert her red apron. "Every daredevil needs a cape," she said with a wink.

He clutched the apron. Think about Robbie Knievel, he thought.

After school most of his class-mates came to watch the big event. The school nurse came to watch Albert in case he fell. While everyone gathered outside, Miss Cruz lined up 20 erasers. Albert waited just inside the double doors, wondering why he'd ever thought being noticed was a good thing.

He saw Miss Cruz look at her watch. "Where's Albert?" she asked, looking around the schoolyard.

Albert drew in a deep breath. He imagined Robbie Knievel lining up his motorcycle to face the Grand Canyon. It was time to face his own canyon. He stepped through the double doors with his red cape swirling behind him.

Everyone began to chant, "Albert! Albert!"

"Are you ready?" asked Miss Cruz.

Albert retied his shoelaces. "Ready," he said, but his legs wobbled like noodles. Remember Robbie Knievel, remember Robbie Knievel, he told himself.

"On your mark, get set, go!" said Miss Cruz.

"Jump, Albert! Jump!" shouted the crowd.

They sounded just like Robbie Knievel's fans. Albert tensed his legs, pushed off the ground, and soared through the air. The school nurse clutched her first-aid kit. The crowd cheered.

Would he make it? Maybe. Maybe not. But suddenly it didn't really matter. He had already achieved his goal: He'd been noticed!

Comprehension Check

1. What does Albert wish for most?

2. Why won't his teacher let him jump 20 phone books on his bike at school?

3. Why do you think it is so important to Albert that the other kids notice him?

4. If you wanted to get noticed in a positive way, what would you do?

Underwear on Parade

by Kathryn Lay

When Mrs. Russell announced, "Bring your favorite collection to school on Monday and find a creative way to display it," Michael knew he could finally show off his underwear collection.

Lots of kids in Michael's class collected things. His best friend, Stephen, collected toy train engines. Patty Parks collected postcards from pen pals around the world. Geraldo Ruiz collected signatures of Hispanics who'd done things he admired.

But Michael collected underwear.

Stephen said, "You can't bring that silly collection to school. Everyone will laugh! They'll make fun of you. You've got to come up with something else before Monday."

"But it's my only collection!" Michael insisted.

Stephen shrugged. "Maybe you could paste leaves in a notebook."

Michael told his friend good-bye and shuffled home. In his room, he opened the box where he kept his collection. He **rummaged** through underwear with stripes, spots, and triangles. He picked up a pair with zoo animals marching across it. He zoomed his favorite pair toward the ceiling, watching the rocket ships that blasted off all over it.

Boxer shorts, briefs, boxer-briefs—he had quite a collection. But how could he display them?

Maybe he could put them on a poster board and talk about the history of underwear. No, he decided. He didn't want to put staples in them.

How about hangers? he thought. He could put them on hangers and hang them around the top of the bulletin board and over the windows. No, he decided. That was too boring.

Then he knew what to do. He called Stephen, who shouted into the phone, "What? Are you nuts? You'll be the biggest joke in fourth grade!"

Michael said he didn't care. "It's my only collection. Besides, I like it. And this way, everyone can see how great they are."

"They'll laugh," Stephen warned.

"It's fun to laugh," Michael said.

"Laugh, laugh, laugh," Stephen sang.

When Monday finally came, Michael was too nervous to eat breakfast. He was glad it was a cold November morning because he could wear a coat. That would help his plan.

Michael felt like a stuffed scarecrow as he thumped to the bus stop and squeezed onto the seat beside Stephen.

"Did you?" Stephen asked.

Michael nodded. Stephen pushed past him and moved to another seat, whispering, "Laugh, laugh, laugh."

After roll call, Mrs. Russell raised her hand for silence. "Okay, everyone," she said. "Let's get started. Michael, please remove your coat in class."

"I can't," he said. "It's part of my collection."

Toby Davis snorted. "You collect coats?"

Michael looked around the room. It was filled with collections. Betty Roberts stood up and talked about her model car collection. Stephen spun three train engines around the tracks on Mrs. Russell's desk. Toby dug snail shells out of a **grubby** paper bag.

"Okay," said Mrs. Russell. "We have time for one more before lunch. Michael, why don't you go next?"

Michael took a deep breath and went to the front of the room. He glanced at Stephen, who slid down in his seat, mouthing, "Laugh, laugh, laugh."

"I, uh, have a very unusual collection," Michael began. He whipped off his coat.

The class **erupted.** Everyone laughed, hooted, hollered, and pointed.

Over Michael's jeans, he wore a thick mound of underwear. Fifteen pairs, to be exact. The top pair was bright blue and covered with giant yellow sunflowers.

Before he could chicken out, Michael lowered the sunflower underwear to the floor. The class got quiet. Students glanced at one another. Some stood up to get a better view. Mrs. Russell **pursed** her lips and clasped her hands in front of her.

As Michael's red, white, and blue underwear appeared, they giggled. Someone started singing "The Star-Spangled Banner." Everyone joined in.

One by one, Michael took off each pair. The Halloween underwear with black cats chasing trick-or-treaters caused everyone to shout, "Boo-tiful!"

The Christmas tree shorts started a chorus of "Jingle Briefs."

When he got to the zoo animal underwear, everyone roared like lions, trumpeted like elephants, or grunted like gorillas. Michael couldn't believe his eyes when he saw Stephen pretending to be a kangaroo.

The last pair of underwear Michael wore over his jeans had jokes printed all over. He took the pair off and passed it around the room.

"Don't worry," he said as Betty held the briefs away with her fingertips. "I never wear anything from my collection. They're all fresh out of the package!"

Everyone laughed again.

"Class, quiet please!" Mrs. Russell said, wiping giggle tears from the corners of her eyes. She turned to Michael. "What a show you've put on!" she said.

Michael looked at Stephen, who stood and saluted.

"I think we can all agree that your collection is the most unusual we've ever seen," said Mrs. Russell. "I haven't had such a good laugh in a long time."

"It was fun!" said Patty Parks.

"And silly," Toby Davis said.

Michael picked up the pile of underwear and stacked it on his desk. Yes, he had the silliest collection around. Stephen was right. Everyone laugh, laugh, laughed. And boy, was it great!

 ## Comprehension Check

1. What is the assignment that starts this story?

2. Why does Michael decide to wear his collection to class instead of displaying it in some other way?

3. What does Michael's friend think of his plan to show off his underwear collection?

4. Everyone laughs, just as Stephen has said they will. Do you think Michael's collection is a success or a failure? Why?

The Zoo in Room 22

by Janice Barrett Graham

Zoe walked into class wearing fuzzy bunny slippers on her feet, but no one in Room 22 stared. The kids in Room 22 were used to Zoe's funny footwear. She wore green alligator slippers or shaggy lion slippers or googly-eyed gorilla slippers.

"Why do you always wear animal slippers?" one of the kids once asked.

"Because they're the closest I can get to having a pet," Zoe said.

When the class did a clay art project, Zoe's was a pet parrot on a perch. When the class wrote Halloween stories, Zoe's was about a pet polar bear on a leash. She was the only one in Room 22 who didn't have a real pet.

"Is there some reason you can't have a pet?" asked her teacher, Mrs. Kindle.

Zoe bit her bottom lip. "No pets are allowed in my apartment building," she said. "Not even a goldfish in a bowl."

On the day Zoe wore her pink pig slippers, a box under her desk wiggled and thumped all through reading. Finally, it was time for show-and-tell. Zoe opened the box and out **slithered** a green snake.

"Ahhh," said the kids in Room 22.

"This is Critter. I found him outside my apartment," said Zoe. "I checked with all my neighbors and he doesn't belong to any of them. Can we keep him in Room 22, Mrs. Kindle?"

Mrs. Kindle let the green snake slide onto her palm. "Yes," she said, "on one condition. Critter will belong to the whole class. Everyone in Room 22 will help take care of him."

Critter stayed, but Zoe still wore animal slippers to school.

On the day Zoe wore her caterpillar slippers, she brought a shoebox that scratched and shuffled all through reading. Finally, during show-and-tell, Zoe opened the lid and out crawled a **tarantula.**

"Oooh!" said the kids in Room 22.

"This is Harry," said Zoe. "I found him in the bathtub. Can we keep him, Mrs. Kindle?"

Mrs. Kindle watched Harry's eight legs carry him across her desk. "Yes," she said, "on one condition."

"We'll take care of him!" everyone said.

Harry stayed, but Zoe still wore animal slippers to school.

On the day Zoe wore her reindeer slippers, she brought a paper bag that didn't make any noise at all. Finally, during show-and-tell, Zoe reached in and pulled out a box turtle with his head tucked inside his shell.

"Oooh!" said the kids in Room 22.

"This is Shelby," said Zoe. "I found him in the park. Can we keep him, Mrs. Kindle?"

Mrs. Kindle saw how quietly Shelby sat in class. "Yes," she said.

Shelby stayed, but Zoe still wore her animal slippers to school.

Now Room 22 had a snake, a tarantula, and a turtle. It wasn't long before Zoe brought in a **parakeet,** a guinea pig, and a **salamander.** She brought a pair of rabbits, three hamsters, a family of white mice, and a bucket of hermit crabs.

One day, the principal visited Room 22. He didn't notice Critter

atop Mrs. Kindle's desk until the snake slithered across his hand.

"Snake!" Principal Walden exclaimed. He backed away from the desk. He put his hand down by the spider box, knocking off its lid. Harry climbed out of the box and crawled up his arm.

"Spider!" yelled Principal Walden, dancing around. He tripped over Shelby, who was **ambling** across the room. Then he fell forward, grabbing the shelf filled with Room 22's pets. The mouse cage tumbled. The hermit crab bucket spilled. Within minutes, the room was filled with fleeing creatures.

"Call an **exterminator!**" shouted Principal Walden.

Mrs. Kindle called the class to order. "It seems we have a zoo in Room 22," she said. "We must find homes for our animals."

The class captured and counted their pets. There were just enough for every person to take one pet home. Zoe hung her head. The bunny ears on her slippers drooped. "Mrs. Kindle?" she asked. "Could I keep my pet in Room 22?"

Mrs. Kindle smiled. "Just one pet?"

Zoe nodded. "Just one pet."

Mrs. Kindle looked at the principal. He nodded.

"Yes," said Mrs. Kindle. "But this time the pet will belong to you. He'll be your responsibility, so you'll have to feed him and clean up after him. Okay?"

"Okay!" Zoe agreed.

Zoe chose Shelby because he always sat quietly in class. The next day, and every day from then on, she wore plain old tennis shoes to Room 22.

 Comprehension Check

1 Why does Zoe wear animal slippers to school?

2 What kinds of animals does Zoe bring to school?

3 How do you think Principal Walden feels about the zoo in Room 22?

4 If your class could have a pet, which kind would you choose? Why?

The Stinky Socks Contest

by Kim T. Griswell

Zach keyed in the address of his favorite Web site. When the page finished loading, the familiar giant eye greeted him with a wink. Zach winked back.

"Hey, dude! What do you have for me today?" Zach asked.

Zach's favorite dotcom featured weekly contests that kids could enter to win cool prizes. Last week a boy from Australia won a computer by naming the capital of every South American country. The week before, a girl from India wrote a poem that won her an all-expenses-paid trip to the theme park of her choice.

He clicked on the lime green contest button and held his breath. A wriggling giant sock came up on the screen. The headline read "Announcing the World's First Stinky Socks Contest!" Zach **scanned** the rules. Entry was open to kids between the ages of eight and 13. In order to win, contestants had to prove their socks were the stinkiest on the planet by sending in a quote from someone who had smelled them. All entries had to be received by midnight in exactly two weeks.

"Whoopee!" Zach shouted as he closed the **browser.** Finally, a contest he could win!

His best friend, Derrick, helped him plan his **strategy.** First, he'd wear the same socks every day for a week. Then he'd take his shoes off in public places and write down whatever comments people made. Someone was bound to say something that would make Zach a winner!

Zach's feet must have been **prime** stinkers because he got his first comment after only two days.

"Zach?" his mom asked when he took his shoes off to watch television. "When is the last time you changed your socks?"

Zach grinned. "I can't change my socks, Mom. I'm in a contest."

"What kind of a contest?" she said, giving him that "here we go again" look.

"A stinky socks contest!"

Zach's mom shook her head. "Well, you win. Go change your socks."

"No, Mom. Really. It's on kidslark.com. First prize is a dirt bike!"

"Zach, if your feet get much worse, Barney will faint!"

Barney was their three-year-old Rottweiler. He was sitting across the room from Zach with his nose tucked under his paw.

Zach laughed. "Good one, Barney!"

He grabbed his journal and wrote down the quote: "Zach's socks are so stinky they could make a Rottweiler faint!"

His next chance for a quote came at the Rock and Roll Burger Barn. When the waitress came to take his order, Zach slipped off his right shoe and waved his foot around.

"Honey," the waitress said, looking down her nose at him. "I hate to be rude, but those socks smell so bad they could wake Elvis from the dead."

"Yes!" Zach stuck his foot back in his shoe and wrote the quote in his journal.

On Saturday, Zach went to Derrick's birthday party. As Derrick's mom passed around plates heaped with chocolate cake and **Neapolitan** ice cream, Zach took off his shoes. Megan Schwartz scrunched up her face. "Mrs. Russell? Make Zach put his shoes back on. His stinky socks are melting my ice cream!"

Zach winked at Derrick. Derrick **glared.** "Not here, Zach. It's my birthday."

Before he put his shoes back on, Zach wrote down the quote.

By the end of the week, he had plenty of great stinky socks quotes. He kicked off his shoes and sat down in front of his computer. He tapped out a rhythm on the desktop as he waited for the Web page to load. When the giant eye winked at him, Zach clicked on the Enter Contest Now button. He filled out the entry form and carefully typed his quotes in the box provided. Then, just as he was about to click on the send button, the screen froze.

"No!" Zach moaned. "Not now!"

He **rebooted** his computer, but instead of the usual smiling computer **icon,** a frowning computer appeared on his desktop. No amount of **trouble-shooting** would make the computer icon smile again. Zach's machine would have to go into the shop.

Zach couldn't believe his luck. After all that work! He might as well forget the contest. Forget the bike. He'd never win now.

Then Zach remembered some-thing. Email wasn't the only way to write to someone. He could send a postcard! He still had three days until the contest ended. That should be enough time for the card to reach kidslark.

On the postcard he wrote,
Dear kidslark.com,
I've been working hard all week to win your Stinky Socks Contest. I hope that you will accept this postcard entry since I can't email you. When I took off my shoes and sat down to send in my quotes, my computer crashed.

He wrote out his quotes, then signed the card, "Your friend, Zach."

After a week in the shop, Zach's computer came home. He booted up and went straight to kidslark. Soon, the giant eye was winking at him once again.

"Hey, dude!" Zach said. "Long time, no see."

He scrolled down the page to find out who had won the contest. The headline read "Stinky Socks Catastrophe!" Zach held his breath as he read the text below the headline.

"Hold your nose, boys and girls. This winner will take your breath away. You may not believe it, but the winner of the Stinky Socks Contest did something really retro! He sent in his winning entry via snail mail! Here it is:

"Zach's socks are so stinky they crashed his computer!"

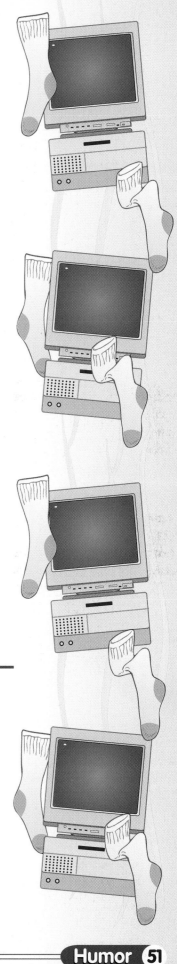

 Comprehension Check

 1 Why does Zach think he can win the Stinky Socks Contest but not the others he mentions?

 2 What is Zach and Derrick's plan to win the contest? Do you think this is a contest-winning strategy? Why or why not?

 3 Do you think stinky socks could really do any of the things people claim Zach's socks do? Why or why not?

4 Zach wears the same socks and takes off his shoes in public places to win the Stinky Socks Contest. What would you be willing to do to win a contest?

Window-Shopping

by Rusty Fischer

Zoom went a passing car. *Honk, honk* sang a speeding bus. The sounds of the big city were nothing new to Timothy and his twin sister, Tina. But even so, they didn't **stray** far from their parents' sides as they looked in the windows of the huge department store.

The store took up a whole city block and gleamed with big, shiny windows that faced the street. Inside each window was a colorful display for window-shoppers to look at. Shoes and dresses and purses and hats seemed to shout from inside each window, "Come inside. Buy me! Come on. What are you waiting for?"

Timothy and Tina's parents just looked at each other and frowned when the children asked to go inside.

"Not today, kids," said their dad.

"We're just looking," said their mom.

There was plenty to look at! "I sure would love to have that set of golf clubs," their mom said. "But my old ones will have to do for now."

Timothy and Tina's dad stopped when he saw a gas grill on sale in another window.

"Wow," said their dad. "What a great grill! Oh well, maybe someday."

The twins didn't see what was so great about staring at golf clubs and a grill. But the minute they stepped in front of the toy store windows, excitement bubbled up in them like fizz in a soda.

"Look at that remote control tank!" Timothy exclaimed. "It's almost as big as the real thing! I bet it's turbo powered! Can I have it? Can I?"

His mom and dad looked at each other and frowned.

"We're window-shopping, remember?" his dad said with a wink. "Maybe some other time, when we can afford it."

"What about that doll?" asked Tina. "The one wearing the ballet costume. All my doll clothes will fit her, and she dances just like a real ballerina."

"Not today, Tina," her mom said. "Maybe we can afford the doll next month."

Although they were disappointed, Timothy and Tina knew better than to **pester** their parents. Their parents would probably get the toys for their birthday next month.

Next month came, but so did more bills. Their parents still couldn't afford the remote control tank and the dancing doll. Timothy got a sweatshirt and socks. Tina got a pair of pants with matching hair barrettes.

Timothy could see that Tina was sad about not getting the doll.

And Tina knew that Timothy still wanted that tank.

Timothy secretly gathered up all of his favorite action figures and went to the houses of his friends.

"What will you give me for these?" he asked, then walked happily away with the money he collected for each toy.

Meanwhile, Tina went to all of her friends to sell her doll clothes. By that afternoon, their pockets were full of money.

"Happy birthday," Timothy said later as he gave Tina her present.

"Happy birthday to you," said Tina, handing him a present.

Tina gasped when she saw the dancing doll. Timothy tore open his present and started playing with the remote control tank he found inside.

"You didn't sell your doll stuff, did you?" Timothy asked.

Tina nodded. "And you sold your action figures," she whispered, her eyes widening.

Timothy threw up his hands. "Now you have the doll," he said, "but you sold all of your doll clothes to buy my tank!"

"Now you have a tank," said Tina, "but you sold all of your action figures to buy my doll!"

"I guess we'll just have to play together," Timothy said with a smile.

 Comprehension Check

 What is special about Timothy and Tina?

 Why don't the twins' parents buy them the toys they want for their birthday?

3 Why do you think the twins give up their favorite toys for each other?

4 What would you do if you wanted to give someone a gift but didn't have the money to buy it?

The Collector

by Pamela Walker

I come from a family of collectors. My dad and mom have 38 salt and pepper shaker sets. Their favorite set is a cowboy pepper kissing a cowgirl salt. My 16-year-old sister collects key chains.

I collect words. When I find a new word I like, I write it on an index card and stick it to my wall. Sometimes I choose a word for the way it looks or sounds, and sometimes because of its meaning.

When my teacher announced that we'd have Collection Day, I was pretty excited. I took 25 of my favorite words off my wall and put them in a recipe box.

The next day I listened to 13 kids share their baseball card collections. There was some argument about favorite players until Mr. Dorset said, "Keep your opinions to yourself." That was fine with me. I had no opinion on ballplayers.

Owen Baker brought his collection of stuff he'd found in garbage cans. He held up a **retainer**, and Maria yelled, "That's mine!" Owen handed it over, and she started to put it in her mouth, but Mr. Dorset stopped her just in time.

Serena Wilcox brought her stamp collection. She had one with a bright yellow fish from the Cayman Islands that looked pretty cool.

Finally it was my turn. I walked to the front with my cards.

"I collect words," I began. "These are my favorites."

I looked around the room. You'd think an ape was sitting on my head the way the kids were staring at me.

"*Aardvark,*" I read. "I like the way the *d* and the *v* sound together." I thought I heard a giggle but chose to ignore it.

"*Obnoxious,*" I read. "That means 'highly **offensive**.'"

"*Zucchini.* That's a kind of green squash, but I don't really like zucchinis. I just selected the word for its sound."

Someone at the back of the room yawned loudly.

What was wrong with everybody? Didn't they appreciate a good word when they heard it? Before I could ask them if they had anything in their *craniums*, the word on my next card, the dismissal bell rang.

As I walked to my seat, Gordy Parker called me a wordy-bird.

I sat by myself on the bus, hoping nobody would bother me, but Patty Mulloni tapped me on the shoulder. She was a baseball card collector, and she wanted to sit with me. I shook my head no.

I guess she didn't get the message because the next thing I knew, she was sitting with me.

"Can I see your collection?" she asked. I just kept looking out the window, hoping she'd go away if I ignored her. From the corner of my eye, I could tell she was writing something.

The bus ride was *interminable*, another favorite word I hadn't been able to share. It means I thought the bus ride would never end. I was glad Patty's stop was first. Finally, in front of my house, I got up and noticed that she'd left a note on the seat. My name was written on the outside in jiggly bus writing. I sat down on my front porch to read it.

Michael,
I have another collection besides baseball cards. I collect bird feathers. I have feathers from 15 different ***species***. *I'll bring them on Monday.*
Patty
P.S. You can have these bird words if you want.
AVIARY*—a big house for lots of birds*
WHIPPOORWILL*—my favorite bird*

I folded the note and put it in my pocket. As I looked down at the walkway, I noticed a brown-speckled feather near my left foot. I picked it up and put it in my pocket too. It was the least I could do in exchange for two new words for my collection.

 Comprehension Check

1 What do most of the students in Michael's class collect?

2 How do you think the other students feel about Michael's collection? What makes you think so?

3 Based on clues in the story, what do you think Michael will do with the feather he finds?

4 What do you collect? Why? If you don't have a collection, what do you think you might be interested in collecting? Why?

The Tasmanian Devil

by Susan Glass

"He spins! He snarls! He shreds things! Best of all, he cracks you up! He's the Tasmanian Devil, a crazy cartoon character. He isn't a real animal. Or is he?" Carey read aloud.

Damian burst into the classroom, spinning like a top. He spun past Mr. Ross's desk. He held his hands up like claws. His tongue hung out of his mouth.

"Damian!" Mr. Ross exclaimed. "Is this part of the report?"

Damian nodded as he spun down the aisle by the windows. He opened all the windows along the way. Then he whirled back up the aisle, shutting the windows as he went.

"Believe it or not, there really is a living, breathing Tasmanian devil," Carey continued. "In fact, there are lots of them. They live in a place called—you guessed it—Tasmania! Tasmania is a large island off the southeast coast of Australia."

By this time, Damian was all spun out.

Carey giggled and said, "I think my partner needs to sit down for a few moments."

Damian sat down in a chair beside a poster filled with cutouts of Australian animals. In the center of the poster was a picture of a Tasmanian devil with its mouth spread wide to show its sharp teeth. Carey continued, "They are a little bit like the cartoon character. They are furry, and they snarl a lot. They have a short tail, a big head, a thick body, and powerful teeth." She pointed to the picture.

"And that's pretty much where the **similarities** end. Real devils don't spin around like my partner. They walk or run on all fours, and they are smaller than you might think. Devils are about the size of a small dog—about a foot tall. A large one could weigh about 26 pounds. Devils are **carnivores**, so they eat meat. They are mainly **scavengers**. This means that they eat dead animals they find."

Damian pulled a plastic rat from his pocket and pretended to eat it.

"Gross!" said someone in the back.

"Devils hunt rats, mice, **reptiles**, **amphibians**, crabs— whatever they can catch or find," Carey said. "They have a great sense of smell."

Damian got down on all fours and began to sniff his way toward the front desks.

"That will do, Damian," Mr. Ross said. "We get the point."

"The sounds Tasmanian devils make are amazing," said Carey.

Damian opened his mouth and screeched so loudly that the principal stuck her head in the door.

"Sorry, Ms. Greene," Mr. Ross said. "We're having a very **dramatic** report on the Tasmanian devil."

Damian snarled, growled, and coughed as if he had a giant hairball in his throat.

Mr. Ross covered his ears as Ms. Greene left.

"Their fierce, scary noises are mostly used to challenge other devils," Carey said. "When one devil wants to challenge another one to fight, he sneezes at him!"

Crinkling up his nose, Damian tried to force a sneeze, but he couldn't. "Guess there's no one I want to challenge right now," he said.

"Tasmanian devils do have a softer side," Carey read. "They are **marsupials**. They have a pouch, much like a kangaroo's. A devil mom usually carries two or three babies in her pouch for about four months. Then the mom leaves them in a simple **den**, such as a hollow log. She looks after them until they can look after themselves."

Damian started to whirl again. He whirled past Mr. Ross's desk, bumped against it, and then whirled into Carey. Carey gave him a push toward the door. He stopped whirling, opened the door, and went outside, rubbing his head.

"So," Carey finished, "the next time you see the Tasmanian Devil cartoon, remember the real devil. He might not be as funny, but he's just as cool!"

 **Comprehension Check**

1 What roles are Carey and Damian playing for their report?

2 What similarities and differences are there between the real Tasmanian devil and the cartoon character?

3 What is Carey talking about when she says the Tasmanian devil has a softer side?

4 What other animals have been made into cartoon characters? What about these characters seems to be based on the real animals? What seems to be imaginary?

Monty's Hot Tub Adventure

by Kim T. Griswell

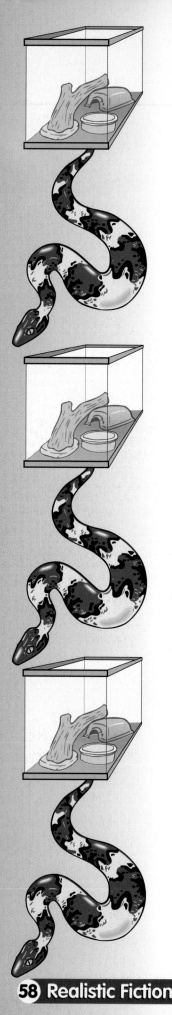

"Rupesh!" Nick yelled. "Monty's missing."

Nick's friend took the stairs two at a time. "What do you mean missing?"

"He's not in his tank. Look," Nick said.

Rupesh crowded in front of the 20-gallon glass tank as Nick lifted the **mesh** lid. He moved aside the tree branch. No Monty. He poked behind the water dish. No Monty. He picked up the plastic hideaway. Still no Monty.

"Come on, Nick," Rupesh said with a laugh. "Where did you hide him?"

Nick shook his head. "I didn't hide him anywhere. He's just gone. We've got to find him before Mom gets home. If she finds out he's escaped, she'll make us move out of the house!" Nick's stomach felt as if he'd just swallowed a five-pound frog.

"He has to be close by," Rupesh said, glancing around the room. "How far could a baby ball python get?"

Nick rolled his eyes. "As far as he wants to. But if he gets outside, he'll die. It's too cold."

Rupesh pushed a stack of reptile magazines off the beanbag chair and plopped into it. "You're the junior **herpetologist**. You're supposed to know everything about **reptiles**. Where should we look?"

Nick thought for a moment.

"Well, he hasn't eaten yet this week."

"Uh-oh." Rupesh nodded **pointedly** across the hall.

Nick nodded. "If he's hungry, he might go after Hannah's gerbil."

"Nah. Monty doesn't even know Hannah has a gerbil. Unless you told him," Rupesh teased.

"I didn't have to tell him anything. If he's hungry, he'll be able to smell the gerbil. **Pythons** pick up smells with their tongues, you know," Nick said. The two friends exchanged looks. "What if Hannah gets home and finds Monty near her gerbil?"

"Let's go!" Rupesh shouted.

They nearly tripped each other rushing to be the first to Hannah's room.

Nick's younger sister kept her gerbil cage in the middle of her bookcase. It was wedged between her copy of *Winnie-the-Pooh* and a stuffed panda she'd gotten at the zoo last year. Nick looked into the cage. George the gerbil wasn't running on his wheel. Where was he?

"There he is!" Rupesh pointed at the gerbil, who was busy nibbling on a piece of carrot tucked into the wood shavings. "We should have known. Monty could never get in there anyway."

Nick raised an eyebrow. "Oh, you'd be surprised. If he was hungry enough, Monty could just climb right up the side of that tank, stick his nose under the lid, and pop it open. Baby pythons are a lot stronger than they look. How do you think he got out of his tank?"

Rupesh slapped his forehead. "I forgot about that," he said. He grabbed Hannah's copy of *Winnie-the-Pooh* and put it on top of the lid. "Just in case Monty does try to get in."

They left Hannah's room and

wandered into the hall. "Okay, junior herpetologist. Where to? That snake of yours is turning out to be a pretty slippery character."

Nick lifted his baseball cap and scratched his head. "Since ball pythons are natives of Africa, they like warm places. Monty seems happiest when his tank is between 80 and 85 degrees. His favorite thing to do is lie in his water dish beneath the heat lamp. It's like his hot tub," Nick said.

Rupesh looked around. "You think he crawled into a **vent**?" He flipped open the hall heating vent and looked inside.

"No. Mom has them all closed. But if you open them up, he might. Then we'd never find him," Nick said.

Rupesh clicked the vent shut. "So where's the warmest place in the house?" he asked.

Nick snapped his fingers. "I know!"

Before Rupesh could ask what he meant, Nick sprinted down the hallway and **clambered** down the stairs. He didn't stop on the main floor but headed down another flight to the basement.

Rupesh hurried to catch up. By the time he reached the bottom of the stairs, Nick had flipped on the light and opened the door to the laundry room.

"You think he's down here doing a load of clothes?" Rupesh asked.

"He's here!" Nick shouted.

"No way," said Rupesh. "How'd you know he'd be in there?"

"Well, I've heard of pythons that will crawl inside a washing machine."

"What for? Do they think it's an amusement park ride or something?"

Nick rolled his eyes. "Of course not. They're attracted to the heat. It's as warm and damp in here as it is in Monty's hot tub. Only bigger!" Nick lifted the caramel, brown, and black snake out of the washing machine. He curled up in a ball in Nick's hand.

"Looks like he's glad you found him."

Nick shook his head. "He's not curling up because he's happy. Ball pythons curl up because they're stressed out. He probably wishes I'd left him right where I found him."

A door slammed upstairs, and Nick's head jerked up. "Mom," he whispered.

"Good thing it was you who found Monty in the washing machine and not your mom," Rupesh whispered back.

"Yeah, or I'd be the one curled up in a ball. Permanently."

He ran a finger along Monty's warm skin. "Time to get you back home, buddy. And no more hot tub adventures."

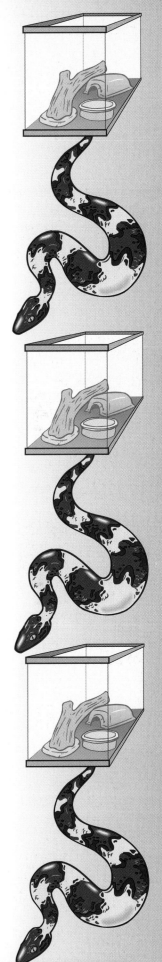

Comprehension Check

1. Rupesh calls Nick a junior herpetologist. Based on clues from the story, what do you think a *herpetologist* might be?

2. Why does Nick think Monty might be in Hannah's room?

3. Why does Rupesh put a book on top of the gerbil cage?

4. If you were Nick, what would you do to make sure Monty does not escape again?

Early Warning!

by Kim T. Griswell

When Sam chased his tail three times and then **sprinted** straight into the sliding glass door like a grizzly bear was chasing him, Bruce knew something was wrong. The eight-year-old collie hadn't run more than a few feet since they'd adopted him from the animal shelter. In fact, all he did was dig holes in the flower beds and snooze in the sun, prompting Bruce's mom to wonder whether they should take him back to the shelter and trade him for a puppy. But Bruce didn't care that Sam was slow and old. He was good company, especially in the afternoons when his mom wasn't home from work.

Sam stood at the door now, not pawing to get in as he usually did, but shaking his great furry head. The tiny dark eyes above his long pointed nose looked **dazed** and confused. Bruce slid open the door. The second it was wide enough, Sam **bolted** through, pushing Bruce back down on the **ottoman** where he'd been sitting watching television.

"Sam? What's wrong, buddy?" Bruce followed him down the hall, reaching his bedroom just in time to see Sam scramble beneath the bed. He hid behind the balls, books, and dirty socks, whimpering.

As Bruce bent down to **peer** at his dog, he heard a loud crack, followed by a low rumble. For a moment, Bruce thought they were testing another rocket at the plant just over the golden hills behind his San Jose **suburb**. Then the floor began to quiver, and Bruce didn't even think before he shoved under the bed beside Sam. As he did, the room started shaking. The **trinkets** on his desk bounced up and down like Mexican jumping beans.

Glass splintered somewhere down the hall. Pots and pans landed with a metallic clang on the kitchen counters. Outside, car alarms whirred and bleeped and moaned. Sam whimpered as the bed started to inch across the floor. Bruce put an arm over him, twining his fingers into the dog's long, silky fur.

"It's okay, buddy. Don't worry," he said, knowing that he was trying to reassure himself as much as Sam. He guessed this was an earthquake—the first one he'd experienced since moving from Ohio to California. He didn't like it. Not at all. Floors were not supposed to roll like something out of a horror movie. Books should sit quietly on their shelves, not fling themselves to the floor in heaps.

Then, as quickly as it started, it was over. Everything stopped crashing and dancing across the room. It felt like he'd been under the bed for hours, but actually less than half a minute had passed. An **eerie** quiet had fallen, broken only by the television **static** sizzling down the hall and the car alarms **wailing** outside.

"Wait here, boy," Bruce motioned for Sam to stay put while he scooted out from under the bed. His knees felt wobbly as he looked around his room. Little league trophies, books, and toys littered the floor.

"What a mess!"

Sam stuck his nose out from under the bed.

"I'll go. You stay right there till I get back." Bruce motioned for Sam to stay. He didn't want him to get glass in his paws.

Bruce stopped when he walked into the living room. He felt like he'd been punched in the stomach. The sliding glass door had shattered into the living room. Giant **shards** of broken glass pierced the ottoman where he'd been sitting moments before the quake hit.

"Bruce!" He turned as his mother slammed through the front door. "I got here as quickly as I could." Her face was white, her eyes **frantic** as she hurried toward him. Before he could say a word, she grabbed him and squeezed him against her. "You're okay!" Her voice was **husky** with tears. "I didn't know if you'd know what to do. I know we talked about it, but..." Her voice trailed off and she let him go just before squeezing the last bit of air from his lungs.

"Mom!" he gulped. "It wasn't me. I didn't know what to do. It was Sam."

"Sam?" Her head turned this way and that as she **surveyed** the damage and looked for the dog.

Bruce nodded. "If it hadn't been for Sam, I'd have been sitting right there when the quake hit." He pointed at the glass-covered ottoman.

His mom reached behind her, feeling for a chair. "I need to sit down," she said. "What did Sam do?"

"He knew it was coming."

His mom shook her head. "How? Scientists don't even know how to predict an earthquake. And you think your dog did?"

Bruce nodded. "My science teacher told us that animals sometimes act weird right before a quake."

"And Sam acted weird?"

"Yep. And he led me back to the bedroom, where we hid under my bed until it was over."

"Where is Sam?"

Bruce led his mother down the hall. Sam was right where he'd left him. The collie lifted his nose when they came in. Bruce's mom knelt and stroked his head.

"Thanks, Sam," she whispered.

"Still want to trade him for a puppy?" Bruce teased.

"Are you kidding? Sam's a hero! Who would want a puppy when we can have an early warning system like Sam instead!"

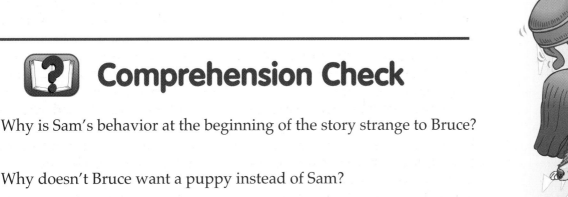

❓ Comprehension Check

1 Why is Sam's behavior at the beginning of the story strange to Bruce?

2 Why doesn't Bruce want a puppy instead of Sam?

3 How does Sam save Bruce from danger?

4 Since Bruce lives in an earthquake-prone area, he needs to know how to stay safe. Where might he get more information about earthquake safety?

The Tooth Fairy Pays a Visit

by Rusty Fischer

Dana Denton was flossing her teeth as she got ready for bed one night when it finally happened: Her loose tooth came out! It had been wiggling for five long days. Now, just like that, it was gone. Finally, she could leave her tooth for the tooth fairy. When she woke up the very next morning, she hoped to find a crisp new dollar waiting for her. She decided to put her tooth in a very special place, one she thought the tooth fairy would **appreciate**. She brushed her teeth (all except one, that is) and hurried off to bed.

Dana was fast asleep when a **shimmering presence** lit up the far corner of her room. There, twinkling like a star, flitted a tiny fairy with brilliant pink wings lined in gold. She held a wand in one hand. A gold silk **pouch** holding many teeth hung from her shoulder.

Dana, tossing and turning in her dreams, didn't even **flinch** as the fairy flitted about her room, lighting it up like a fireworks display.

The tooth fairy glided over to peek under Dana's fluffy pillow. Although she searched and searched, there was no tooth to be found.

"Well, that just can't be!" whispered the tooth fairy. "My missing tooth alarm went off just moments ago. I'm positively sure I'm at the right place!"

Determined to find the missing tooth (it *was* her job, after all), the tooth fairy flitted silently around Dana's room. She peeked under the clothes folded neatly on a chest at the foot of the bed. She poked among the stuffed animals stacked carefully on a shelf, but there was not a tooth to be found. Had Dana's tooth just gone poof?

Next, the tooth fairy flew into Dana's closet. The clothes hung in neat rows, sorted by colors. She peeked in the pocket of a white shirt. No tooth. She poked in the pocket of a green skirt. No tooth. She lifted the lid of the laundry hamper and poked her wand into the clothes piled inside. Still no tooth.

"Don't kids know you're supposed to put your tooth beneath your pillow?" she muttered. "It says so right there on page 1 of the *Tooth Fairy Manual*!"

She flew out of the closet and **flitted** back and forth, tapping her cheek with her glowing wand. Where could it be? Where could it be? Usually when she couldn't find a tooth it was because the child's room looked like a tornado had whipped through it. Not even the best fairy could find a tooth in a mess. But this room wasn't messy. It was the neatest room she'd ever seen.

"Now, if I were a very neat

little girl who'd just lost my tooth," murmured the tooth fairy, "where would I hide it?"

An idea lit up the fairy's face. "Of course," she said as she zipped toward the bathroom.

On the counter beside the sink, she found a glass of mouthwash. She flew over the glass and peered inside. There, resting at the bottom of the glass, was the missing tooth.

The tooth fairy shook her head and smiled. "I should have known," she said. She pulled out a string of dental floss, stretched it across the counter, and waved her magic wand over it. Then she left Dana's reward beside the glass and flew off with the minty-smelling tooth in her gold silk pouch.

The next morning, Dana found not one, but two crisp new dollar bills on the bathroom counter. Beside the bills, she found a message written with dental floss. "For the cleanest tooth in town."

Comprehension Check

1 What are some of the places Dana's visitor looks for her missing tooth?

2 Based on details in the story, what kind of girl do you think Dana is?

3 Why do you think the tooth fairy says she should have known where Dana put her tooth?

4 In what special place would you hide a tooth for the tooth fairy?

The Story Collector

by Kim T. Griswell

She'd been there for as long as Kateke could remember, sitting on the corner beneath the green-and-white-striped **awning**. The Enchanter's Dream, a used-book store, specialized in rare and hard-to-find books. Kateke usually tried to ignore the odd old woman, who wore a tall blue magician's hat woven with twinkling silver stars. Her patched blue velvet cloak barely reached around the folds of her stomach. Her thin cheeks glowed pink as **posies**, but her eyes were gray, nearly white, so that the pupils looked like black freckles on pale skin.

The kids in the neighborhood called her the story collector. If you told her a story and she liked it enough to write it down, she paid five whole dollars for it. She claimed she wrote books for children and she was always looking for new stories to share, but Kateke thought there was more to it than that. For one thing, whenever kids sold stories to the old lady, they could no longer remember them. It was as if those stories had vanished out of their minds forever, as if those things had never happened to them. For another, although she knew that the story collector's real name was Sadie Zazel, Kateke couldn't find any of her books in the library or on any online bookstores.

Though all of Kateke's friends had sold stories to the lady, Kateke refused. She clutched her stories deep in her heart or scribbled them in her journal. Somehow, she sensed that they were too important to sell for

five dollars.

Today was different. Today was her mother's birthday, and she hadn't been able to collect enough cans to sell to buy her mom the present she'd had in mind. Her mother needed a new pair of gloves. Driving a taxi could be cold work in the winter.

"One day my fingers are going to freeze right to the steering wheel!" her mom would say.

The coins in Kateke's pockets made her jeans sag, but they only added up to $9.95. She needed another five dollars for the fur-lined leather gloves at the department store uptown.

That's why Kateke found herself in front of The Enchanter's Dream. She stood staring at the weird old lady, wondering what would really happen to her story if she sold it. She'd chosen one of her favorites because she knew the story collector only paid five bucks for the best. When her mother was about 18 years old, she worked as a **dispatcher** for a cab company. She answered phones and then radioed the drivers, telling them where to pick up passengers. One day, a driver called in sick. Since the drivers made more each day in tips than her mom made in a week from her salary, she wanted to become a driver, but the owner of her company had a policy. No women drivers. He thought it was too dangerous.

Kateke's mom had convinced him to give her a try. She'd made more money for the company that day than any other driver's best day. The rest was history, or "herstory," as her mom liked to say.

Kateke marched up to the story collector before she lost her nerve. "Before I tell you anything, I want to know why none of my friends can remember their stories once they've sold them to you."

The story collector wiped at an ink smudge on the tip of one **gnarled** finger. Her pale eyes seemed to look deep inside Kateke.

"Well, well." A grin tickled her pink cheeks. "You noticed that, did you?"

Kateke's eyes narrowed. She nodded **warily**.

"Most kids don't pay the least bit of attention to their stories." She shifted on her stool, tucking the cushion back under her. "They don't seem to care whether they remember the stories they tell me or not."

"Well, I care." Kateke couldn't keep the heat from her voice.

"I'll tell you a secret," the story collector said, motioning her closer.

Kateke stepped **hesitantly** toward her.

"If your story really means something to you, if you've got it nestled down here," she tapped Kateke's chest, "it won't disappear when you tell it to me. But if it's not woven tightly inside you like the silver threads in my cap," she said, "it will **unravel** with each stroke of my pen and you'll have lost it forever."

She dipped her quill pen into a pot of night-black ink, then held it for a moment above a blank page in a blue leather book.

"Well?" she asked.

Kateke thought of her mom's frozen fingers on that cold steering wheel every morning. Then she thought about the young girl who was her mother, convincing the owner of the cab company that she could do more than just tell other cabbies where to pick up a **fare**. That story was a part of what made her mom who she was. Tough. Hardworking. A woman Kateke admired more than any other. A woman who deserved a pair of warm, fur-lined gloves for her birthday. Those were things that Kateke could never forget. She drew a deep breath, then nodded. "It all began like this.…"

Comprehension Check

1. What makes Kateke suspicious of the story collector?

2. Why do you think the cab company owner lets Kateke's mother keep driving after the day she substituted for the sick driver?

3. According to the story collector, why do Kateke's friends not remember their stories once they've sold them to her?

4. Do you think Kateke will remember her story once she tells it? Why or why not?

The Pocket Dragon

by Kim T. Griswell

When Kelsey wished for a dragon to help get her big brother off her back, she was expecting something about 12 feet tall with fiery breath and sharp claws.

"What would you have me do?" the dragon asked when it puffed into **existence**.

"Oh, no!" Kelsey plopped down on her bed and put her purple velvet pillow over her eyes. "I didn't ask for a flying **chameleon**! I asked for a dragon."

The tiny dragon floating about two feet above her head had big googly eyes and whiskers like a catfish. Its scales shimmered from green to rose to purple, then back again.

"I did not come across the world to be insulted!" The dragon hissed and its pink nostrils **flared**. "I suppose you were expecting one of those great big British dragons."

Kelsey tossed the pillow on the floor and sat up. "Of course. I've got a pesky BIG brother, not a pesky little brother."

"Well, I'm not a British dragon. I'm a Chinese dragon. In case you didn't know, dragons can be big enough to fill the sky, or small enough to fit in your pocket."

"So I get a pocket dragon." Kelsey rested her elbows on her knees and her chin on her palms.

"If I am not needed, I will go back to my chess game with the **emperor**." The dragon turned black; its eyes glowed golden.

"No!" Kelsey held up a hand. "If you're the only dragon I can get, then you'll have to do."

The dragon crossed its **forelegs** and turned its back on her; its tail twitched angrily.

"I mean, you're the most amazing dragon I've ever seen." She crossed her fingers behind her back.

"I see that," said the dragon.

Kelsey uncrossed her fingers. "Really. You're fabulous. Wonderful. Magnificent!"

"That's better." The dragon's wings fluttered and it sank onto her comforter, curling up in a ball. "I am Jing-wei." The dragon bowed its head.

Kelsey bowed back.

"Tell me your problem."

"My big brother is driving me nuts! He plays music so loud that I can't concentrate on my reading." She held up her favorite book: *Harry Potter and the Sorcerer's Stone.* "He hides my homework. And," she leaned forward, "he makes fun of my clothes. Can you believe that?"

The dragon's whiskers twitched as if it were trying to hide a smile.

"What?" Kelsey looked down at her tie-dyed T-shirt, red bell-bottoms, and bright yellow socks.

"Nothing, child. It's just that, no matter what you wear, your brother will tease you. That's what big brothers do."

"Now you sound like my mother." Kelsey pouted.

"Mothers are very wise." The dragon blinked.

"Okay, so what *can* you help me with?"

"I can help you fight fire with fire."

"You're not going to deep-fry him, are you? I mean, it's a good idea, but I don't think my parents would be too happy."

"Of course not. You're getting me confused with those British dragons again. Chinese dragons use their great wisdom to defeat their enemies. When I say 'fight fire with fire,' I mean do to your brother what he has done to you. Only better." Its snout curled back in a smile and a long forked tongue zipped out.

Jing-wei disappeared for a few seconds. When it returned, it held a CD in its forepaws. "When your brother plays his music tonight, put this on your stereo and turn up the volume."

Kelsey had never heard Chinese singers. The ones on Jing-wei's CD screeched like fingernails on a chalkboard. "They actually listen to this stuff in China?"

Jing-wei nodded. "It is very beautiful, but I have heard that Westerners do not care for it."

Later that evening, Adam burst into Kelsey's room. "Turn down that noise!" he demanded.

Jing-wei darted under a pillow.

"Not until you turn yours down!" Kelsey replied. "Every time you turn that stuff up loud enough to bug me, I'm going to play my new favorite CD." She folded her arms and grinned.

Adam's face turned the color of cherry pie as he stormed out of the room. After a few minutes, his music stopped pounding on her wall.

"We did it!" Kelsey teased Jing-wei out from under the pillow. "Not bad for a pocket dragon."

The next morning, as Kelsey gulped down a glass of orange juice, Adam **thrust** a social studies worksheet in her face.

"What's this?" he demanded.

Kelsey looked at the page. Spiky purple pawprints wandered across Adam's careful cursive answers.

"Dragon prints?" she asked.

"That's not funny," he said. "I worked hard on this stuff and now I'll lose points because you pulled this silly stunt!"

Kelsey looked him in the eye. "How does it feel?"

Adam blinked. He looked away. "Yeah, I get the message. You keep your paws off my homework and I'll stay away from yours."

"Deal!" Kelsey grinned. She rushed back up to her room to thank Jing-wei.

"I'll never get this off my paws!" Jing-wei complained.

Kelsey laughed.

"What is so funny?" Its forked tongue **lolled** out of its mouth, covered with purple ink from licking its paws.

Kelsey held up a mirror.

Jing-wei's laugh sounded like a tinkling bell. "A small price to pay for a successful ending," it said. "But now that your problem is solved, I must say good-bye." The dragon bowed its head.

"Do you have to go?" Kelsey asked.

Jing-wei nodded. "I have a chess game to win!" It sprang into the air, wings sparkling. "But if that brother of yours gets out of line again, I'll return. That is, if you will settle for a pocket dragon!"

"I'd rather have a small, wise dragon than a big fiery one any day!" Kelsey grinned.

Comprehension Check

1 When Jing-wei first appears, why is Kelsey disappointed?

2 What is Jing-wei's plan to stop Adam from bothering his sister?

3 Why must Jing-wei leave once Kelsey's problem is solved?

4 Tiny Jing-wei uses wisdom to solve Kelsey's problem. If a big fire-breathing dragon came to Kelsey's aid, what do you think it would do?

The Case of the Pilfering Parrot

by Kim T. Griswell

"Hey! That bird just stole my diamond earring!"

Nelson turned just in time to see a bright green and blue parrot spread its wings and fly off his mother's shoulder.

At last, he thought. A case for the great junior detective!

"Don't worry, Mom!" he yelled. "I'll catch that thief!"

The parrot swooped down an alley. Nelson was in hot **pursuit**. When the bird dipped around the corner, Nelson feared the **pilfering** parrot would get away. He sped up, skidded around the corner, and then stopped. Where was that bird?

He caught a glimpse of flashing green and blue feathers flying through an open window in an apartment building. Nelson counted four floors up and three windows away from the center of the building.

Once inside, Nelson took the stairs two at a time. Once he reached the door, he paused. He couldn't just say, "Turn over that pilfering parrot, or I'm calling the police!" No, first he had to find some proof. And to find proof, he had to get inside.

Nelson thought for a moment. His school was having a paper drive. That would give him an excuse to knock on the door.

His knock brought a slow, **cautious** answer. The door opened as far as the chain would allow, and a sweet face peered out.

"Yes?" the elderly woman asked. "What do you want, young man?"

Nelson cleared his throat. "Good day, ma'am. My school is having a paper drive. I was wondering if you would like to donate any old newspapers."

"Why, yes, I would," she said. "Just a minute."

She closed the door. Nelson heard the chain rattle; then the door opened wide.

"Come in, young man. Come in."

Nelson stepped through the door and checked out the room. Stacks of old newspapers **teetered** on every surface.

Nelson gulped.

"I'll just find some bags for you to load those in," the woman said.

The great junior detective could have bitten his tongue. Why'd I have to tell her about the paper drive? he wondered. Now he'd be here all day gathering papers.

In a few minutes, she came back with a stack of brown paper bags.

"There you are," she said. "Take all you want."

Nelson started stuffing papers into the bags.

"Just leave me a little stack," she said with a smile. "I need them to line Petey's cage."

Nelson perked up. "Petey?" he asked.

She nodded. "My parrot."

So the thief was nearby.

"Would you like to meet him?" she asked.

"Sure!" Nelson exclaimed. This was his chance.

"In here." She motioned him into a room.

Nelson stepped inside. A bright green and blue blur streaked toward him and landed on his shoulder.

"Oh!" The elderly woman clapped. "Petey likes you!"

The bird shifted from foot to foot, pricking Nelson's skin with its sharp claws and pecking at his earlobe.

"Petey, get off the young man. Don't you see you're hurting him?" she **scolded**.

Petey flapped his wings and squawked but stayed on Nelson's shoulder. Great, Nelson thought. I came here to capture a thief, and instead he's captured me.

"Petey! Off!" the woman insisted.

Finally the bird flew off and headed for the perch in his cage.

"Such a well-trained bird, don't you think?" she asked.

Too well trained, thought the junior detective.

"Did you train Petey yourself?" he asked.

"Oh, no." She shook her head. "My neighbor Murray Applebaum trained him," she continued, "before he went away to the big house!"

"The big house?" Nelson asked.

"Prison, young man," she replied. "They found a **stash** of stolen jewelry in his apartment. He kept saying he didn't steal anything. Poor Murray." She shook her head. "Caught red-handed and still trying to claim innocence."

"Ma'am," Nelson said, "I think Murray might have been telling the truth. *He* probably didn't steal anything."

Nelson marched over to the cage and peered inside. "But Petey did!" he said, pointing at Petey.

"What? Petey? Young man, Petey couldn't possibly be a thief," said the woman.

"Then what is that diamond earring doing in his dish?" Nelson asked.

"Diamond earring! What diamond earring?" She looked into the cage. Then she stuck a finger into the dish, pushing aside the seeds. The shiny earring sparkled.

"Oh, Petey! What have you done?" she cried.

"He snatched that right off my mother's ear!" Nelson said.

"Why, Murray must have trained him to do that." She put a hand to her cheek and shook her head in disbelief.

"You won't turn Petey in, will you?" She blinked uncertainly.

Nelson shook his head. "No, ma'am. If you promise to keep that window closed from now on." He pointed to the open window in Petey's room.

"I promise," she said.

Nelson walked into the hallway, whistling. Case closed. The great junior detective had done it again.

"Oh, young man!" the woman called after him.

Nelson turned. "Yes?"

"You forgot your papers."

 ## Comprehension Check

1 What starts Nelson on his search for the jewel thief?

2 Why do you think Nelson wishes he hadn't told the elderly woman about his school's paper drive?

3 Based on clues in the story, what do you think the word *pilfering* means?

4 Nelson thinks of himself as a junior detective. What do you imagine yourself to be?

 Suspense **69**

Tracks in the Sand

by Pamela Love

Finding my five-year-old sister on the crowded beach wasn't easy. I wished she'd stayed closer to Mom's umbrella. Finally I spotted her, but she didn't answer when I called, "Tara, come on!"

As I headed toward her, I accidentally knocked over some plastic chess pieces circled around the sand castle behind hers. "Sorry," I apologized. The boy stood them up again, pressing their round bases down more firmly in the sand. Those knights must be guarding his castle, I thought.

Silent, but **pouting**, Tara followed me back to Mom. Then she burst out, "My castle's no good. It's just a sandpile. Some kids are making real-looking castles with plastic things." She pointed at red and blue tower **molds** scattered around the beach.

"Tara, today's been tough for me too," Mom sighed. "My earring fell apart."

"Did you lose the pearl?" I asked. Grandma had left Mom those pearl earrings. I knew how much they meant to her.

"No, luckily. Both pieces fell right here. I knotted them in my handkerchief." Patting her beach bag, she said, "I'll take them to a jeweler on Monday."

"Can we go into town now?" Tara begged. "You could go to the jewelry store, and then you could get me a castle-making thing."

"Mom! I wanted to sketch bird tracks this afternoon," I said. "If we go into town now I won't have time before we have to leave."

"Chris is right. Let's just enjoy the beach while we're here," Mom said.

"You and your old tracks." Tara **glared** at me. "What good are a bunch of old bird tracks, anyway?"

My face grew hot as I picked up my logbook. Tara didn't understand why I was always collecting animal tracks. She didn't understand that tracks were like clues. Just by looking at the tracks, I could tell what kinds of animals had been in a place.

"Look, maybe there's another way to make your castle better," I said. "Maybe you could decorate your castle with shells."

"Maybe," Tara said.

"Well, I'll see you later!" I called as I headed down the beach.

I sketched gull tracks and **sandpiper** tracks. I sketched dog tracks and toddler tracks. I even sketched something that looked like crab tracks. When it started sprinkling, I headed back to our umbrella. No one was there.

"Over here, Chris!" Mom called.

She and Tara were near the ocean's edge, digging through sand castles. Tara was crying.

"What's wrong?" I asked.

"Tara lost my earring," Mom

answered sadly.

I couldn't believe it. "Tara! You took Mom's earring?"

Tara sniffed. "I wanted my castle to be special, so I turned Mom's handkerchief into buried treasure. I dug a hole right in the center of my castle so I would know where to find it later. Then I wanted a soda and we had to go to the bathroom, and—"

Mom interrupted, "Now we can't find her sand castle! Do you remember which one was hers?"

Shaking my head, I stared at the beach. The sand castle kingdom had grown while I sketched tracks. Castles dotted the beach as far as I could see. The castle builders had left their castles to the rain. How would we ever find Tara's?

As I wandered along the shore, I could see that the tide was rising. Every wave that came up smoothed out more of the beach, carrying sand back to the water. Castles were disappearing. The "treasure" might already be in the ocean.

Closing my eyes, I tried picturing Tara's sand castle. All I could see was a pile of sand until I re-membered the boy with the chess pieces. "Tara, is the earring in the castle you were building before lunch?" I asked.

She nodded.

Maybe the boy had left a chess piece behind. I **crisscrossed** the beach, but either the boy had taken all the chess pieces or the waves had. I sighed. If only plastic knights left tracks like animals. As I thought about tracks, an image of fallen chess pieces and circles in the sand flashed into my mind. That was it!

I dashed from castle to castle. Finally I stopped, looking down at one. I dug into the castle in front of it until I pulled out the handkerchief. The broken earring was still inside. "I've got it!" I called.

Mom hugged me so hard I had trouble explaining about the chess pieces.

Confused, Tara said, "But they're gone now."

I pointed. "See all the little circles around this castle? The chess pieces had round bases."

Tara's mouth went round with surprise. "You found their tracks!"

I nodded, then grinned. "And they led me right to the treasure."

❓ Comprehension Check

1 Why doesn't Chris want to leave the beach to go into town?

2 Why does Tara take her mother's earring?

3 What do you think is Chris's favorite subject in school? Why?

4 What, if anything, do you think Tara learns from this experience?

Tunnel Vision

by Kim T. Griswell

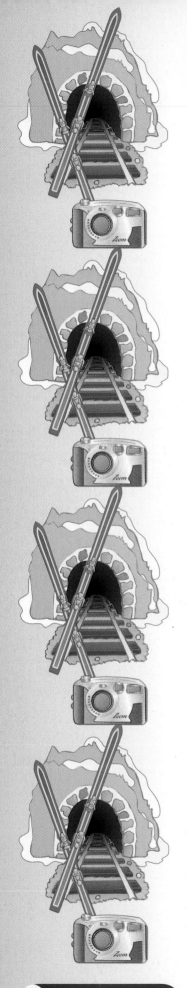

By the time the morning train to the ski lodge left the station, the **frayed** wires had already begun to spark. None of the holiday travelers juggling their skis, boots, and luggage noticed the wisp of smoke coiling like a snake beneath the train's engine.

Chief, who'd gotten her nickname from the hours she spent watching her dad fight fires, might have noticed if she hadn't been busy worrying about whether she'd end up rolling like a snowball to the bottom of the bunny slope. She had followed her classmates onto the train with mixed feelings. Claire Dukes had been teasing her all morning.

"I've got my camera ready, so be sure to let me know when you take your first run," she said. Her buddies giggled. They'd all had plenty of practice, but Chief's firefighter dad was a single parent. He couldn't afford to **splurge** on ski trips. In fact, if their class hadn't raised the money for this trip, Chief wouldn't even be here. Suddenly, she wished she hadn't sold so many candy bars.

"Stop worrying," said her best friend, Drew. "You look like you're going to take a math test, not going on a trip to the hottest ski slope in Colorado."

Chief scrunched up her nose. "I know, I know." She tried to relax as they left the gingerbread town and headed into hills covered with firs and pines.

Under the train, the cold wind whipped the snake until a red tongue of flame shot from its mouth. Wires crackled and hissed.

"Do you smell something?" Chief asked, turning in her seat to **scan** the car. A hot, **metallic** taste clung to her tongue. She tried to swallow it, but it settled there like fuzz from a cold.

Drew snuggled into her pillow. "No."

Chief couldn't get the smell of hot metal off her mind. As the train rounded a corner and swooped into a tunnel, she wondered if she should tell the conductor or the engineer.

Beneath the train, the flame had grown, **engulfing** wires and melting plastic. The snake wound its way upward to **peer** into Chief's window.

Chief could wait no longer. She jumped over Drew and raced down the car to pound on the glass separating her from the engineer.

He opened the door and scowled. "Get back in your seat, please, Miss."

"There's a fire!" she said.

The engineer turned quickly to his instrument panel. No red warnings blinked in the dim light. He shook his head.

"But I saw smoke."

As she spoke, a red light began to **pulse** on the panel. The engineer gasped. "Go sit down. I've got to stop the train."

Air brakes brought them to a stop, nearly knocking Chief from her feet as she hurried back down the aisle.

Within seconds, the engineer came into the first car. "Stay calm, everyone, and please exit from the train as quickly as possible."

The noise level began to rise as travelers sprang from their seats. Some hurried toward the exits; others **fumbled** for their luggage.

"Leave everything," the engineer said as he hurried toward the next car.

Drew turned a sleepy face toward Chief. "What's going on?"

"There's a fire," Chief whispered.

"Fire!" Drew shrieked, her shrill voice cutting through the confusion. Soon other voices rose, and the cry of fire fled from car to car. Confused and frightened people crammed into the narrow aisle. Chief knew what panicked people could do.

"Everyone stay calm," she shouted, keeping her voice **confident**. "There's plenty of time."

Those in the other cars kept fighting toward the doors, but Chief saw her classmates turn toward her. Even her teacher, Mr. Michels, seemed ready to listen. With Chief directing, they managed to safely empty the first car.

Once outside, Chief saw the fire. It streamed beneath the train and began to lick the side panels. She could see the conductor pointing people toward the end of the tunnel they'd entered only a few minutes earlier. Under his guidance, the frightened passengers from the other cars began to run back down the track.

Chief turned toward the other end of the tunnel. It loomed dark and **ominous** as the train's headlights faded, but the smoke that began to **billow** from beneath the cars chased the fleeing passengers.

"Wait!" Chief yelled. "Don't go that way!" Some people kept running, but others hesitated and turned.

Drew caught her elbow. "What are you saying? You want us to head into that!" She pointed into the darkness.

"Look at the way the smoke is blowing," Chief said. "If we go that way, the smoke will **suffocate** us before we make it out."

The other passengers milled around, uncertain. "The conductor wants us to go that way; I think we should follow him," said an elderly man. Sweat beaded on his bald head, and he backed away from the train. Others nodded and started to head toward the faint light, which now looked hazy, smoky.

"Wait!" Mr. Michels stepped forward. "Her father's a firefighter. We should listen to her."

Wary, but too frightened to argue, the others backed away from the lighted end of the tunnel and followed Chief into the darkness. The minute they got beyond the engine, she tasted cleaner air. It gave her confidence as she instructed everyone to clasp hands and walk quickly. Only a few stumbles and sobs broke the silence. Chief's stomach felt as tight as if she'd just done a hundred sit-ups, but the farther they went, the clearer the air felt. Soon, the fire's heat faded and cool air began to **waft** over them. Then a half circle of light appeared ahead.

"We're gonna make it!" someone—it sounded like Claire—yelled.

When they stumbled into the light, the whole class surrounded Chief, crying and hugging and thanking her.

Claire held up her camera. "Hey, Chief! How about a picture?" she asked.

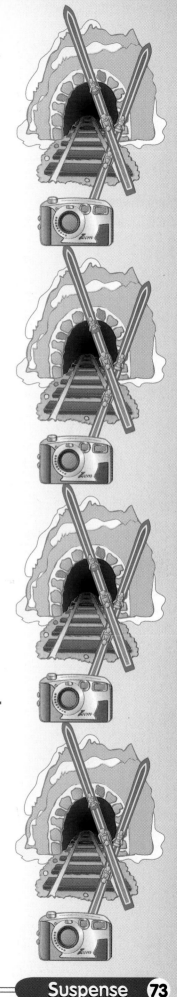

❓ Comprehension Check

1 Why is Chief worried about the ski trip?

2 Why doesn't Chief know how to ski?

3 What clues make Chief think there might be a fire on the train?

4 How does Chief know which direction will lead to safety?

The Circus Screamer

by Kim T. Griswell

Cole wasn't sure why he always avoided the roller coaster that disappeared into the clown's **gaping** grin. Maybe it was because a friend told him a spooky tale about a group of high school seniors who rode the coaster into the jaws of the Circus Screamer but never came back out. He figured that the tale was just like lots of others—purely imaginary. The park would have shut the ride down if that had really happened. Still, something about the ride gave him the shivers. Give him the Ferris wheel or the Parachute Drop or the River Blast anytime!

He almost wished he hadn't volunteered to take his young cousin, Brad, to the park to keep him out of their parents' hair while they visited. It was the last weekend before the park shut down for winter and way too chilly for the water rides. A **brisk** breeze rocked the Ferris wheel. Now Brad was tugging Cole toward the Circus Screamer and what could he say? Sorry, kid. I know you want to ride the coaster, but I'm scared. No way.

So Cole threaded through the empty iron **maze** toward the clown's mouth, wishing there was a long line to wait behind so he could prepare himself for the ride. Unfortunately, only two kids blocked their way onto the coaster. At least they would take the front seats in the car and he wouldn't have to be the first one into that yawning throat. But they didn't, and before Cole knew it, Brad was dragging him toward the front car. The young boy's hand felt warm, making Cole realize how cold and **clammy** his own hand was.

"Why don't we catch a seat in the middle?" Cole suggested. He planted his feet to stop Brad's forward movement.

"What's the matter?" Brad's brows raised over a crooked grin. "Ya scared?"

Cole quickly shook his head but couldn't stop his knees from shaking. He followed Brad into the car, then started fumbling with the seat belt. When the cold metal catch clicked together over his stomach, he felt trapped. Now there was no way out. The clown's **monstrous** red lips **loomed** close, ready to swallow him in one gulp. With a rattle and a clank, the coaster began to move forward.

Brad whooped and raised his hands. "Here we go!"

The coaster clicked as slow as a snail up the first hill, then dropped. Cole's stomach jumped into his throat. He gulped it back down and tried to remember to breathe.

"Yee-haw!" Brad yelled.

Backlit circus animals jumped out of the coal black tunnel. A Bengal tiger sprang at his face, claws bared. An elephant raised a giant foot to crush the car. He closed his eyes and whispered to himself, "It's just a ride." His stomach began to turn flips.

Cole opened his eyes just as the coaster tilted to the right and whipped sideways, jerking a knot into his neck.

Brad slid toward him on the seat, slamming him into the side of the car. His hip crunched into the metal, sending a shooting pain up his side just as they came out of the turn and **plummeted** into total darkness.

Chilly air made his breath freeze in his throat.

Beside him, Brad had grown quiet. Cole could feel tension in the younger boy's **posture**. He was as stiff as a fishing rod.

"W-what's that?" he whispered, leaning toward Cole.

Up ahead, something that looked like a **luminous** raging river streamed across the track. It looked like if they kept going straight, they'd be **submerged**. Beside him, Brad started to whimper. Cole managed to pull one hand off the bar and put his arm around his cousin. He did his best to **reassure** Brad.

"It'll be okay. Just wait. We'll turn before we get there," Cole said. But fear made it difficult for him to believe that. In his mind, he saw a crowd of misty teens near the river, waving their hands in warning.

He heard ghostly voices yell, "Go back!" Then Cole felt the car slam into something. The two boys were thrown back in their seat. The air was forced out of their lungs. A blast of **frigid** air and cold water splashed over them. Brad coughed and gulped beside him.

"Hang on, buddy!" Cole spluttered.

Then, amazingly, the coaster swung sharply, skimming the edge of the river and turning left. They rounded a corner as if on two wheels and burst into sunlight.

Cole blinked. His jeans were soaked on the right side. Brad's hair was plastered to his forehead. He turned owl-wide eyes on Cole.

Cole flung his head back, showering Brad with water. "What a ride!" Cole yelled, grinning. "Want to go again?"

❓ Comprehension Check

 Why is Cole afraid to ride the Circus Screamer?

 Why don't the two boys have to wait long to board the ride?

 How does Brad feel about the ride before it starts compared to how he feels as they near the river?

4 How do Cole's feelings about the ride change? Why?

Answer Keys

Page 5

1. The cap is special to Dirk's dad because he was wearing it when his team won the California Coastal Marathon.
2. Students' responses will vary. One possible response: The crabbers probably couldn't pull the little girl to safety without Dirk's help because they didn't have the strength.
3. The weather caused Dirk to lose his cap, but it helped to save the little girl's life. It made him stop, and that's when he noticed what was happening.
4. Allow for discussion.

Page 7

1. Uncle Owen has so many swamp stories because he was born and raised in the Okefenokee Swamp.
2. Jim thinks he sees hundreds of alligators floating in the open water, but they turn out to be lily pads.
3. Students' responses will vary. One possible response: It is probably not safe for them to leave the campsite without their parents because there are too many dangerous things, such as alligators, in a swamp.
4. Allow for discussion.

Page 9

1. Lindsey thinks that because Mrs. Mudgeon's home is beside a vacant lot, she should expect to have balls kicked into her yard sometimes.
2. They think Lindsey has a problem with her temper because she calls Mrs. Mudgeon a "mean woman" and yells at others.
3. Students' responses will vary. Possible responses: Lindsey might have apologized instead of shouting. She might have played at the park as Mrs. Mudgeon requested. She and her friend might have been more careful and not kicked the ball into Mrs. Mudgeon's yard.
4. They both have bad tempers. Students' responses to the second part of the question will vary. Accept all reasonable responses.

Page 11

1. Ryan's mother has found the map in a box of his father's belongings.
2. They find a rotted wooden post that may have been a sign marking the trail.
3. They are worried because the trail is not well marked, the sun is going down, and walking will take longer than riding. They may not be able to find their way out.
4. The bike his father has left in the clubhouse saves the day.

Page 13

1. They are looking for gold.
2. Miguel has heard that there are wacky prospectors around who will chase people who try to jump their claims. They are afraid that he might chase them.
3. They start a landslide and throw their pans into it so he will think they've been killed.
4. The prospector follows them because there are dangerous animals in the woods, such as mountain lions and grizzlies, and he wants to make sure they are safe.

Page 15

1. Red goes onto Mr. Cooper's porch because he sees some sunflower seeds and he wants a snack.
2. When Red lives in the wild, he plays with his squirrel brothers and sister. He hunts for food and stores spruce cones for the winter. In captivity, Mr. Cooper feeds Red. Red drinks from a water bottle and exercises by running around his cage.
3. Students' responses will vary. One possible response: Mr. Cooper probably lets Red go free because he feels bad when Red's tail breaks and he realizes that Red doesn't want to be tamed.
4. Allow for discussion.

Page 17

1. Grover decides to feed vitamins to the lizard because he knows that his brother takes vitamins to make him strong. He thinks they might help the lizard.
2. Students' responses will vary. One possible response: Brad is a healthy person. He jogs and takes vitamins, prompting Grover to call him a health nut.
3. Students' responses will vary. One possible response: The parts about finding the lizard and buying it vitamins from the pet store seem real. The part about the giant talking lizard seems like a dream.
4. Allow for discussion.

Page 19

1. Keelo is a green turtle.
2. Keelo scurries down the beach toward the sound of the surf, then swims out to sea.
3. Keelo comes back to lay eggs.
4. Students' responses will vary. Possible responses: Crabs and birds will eat some of them before they get to the water. Fish will eat some of the ones that make it to the water. Some of them will find their way to the seaweed where they can grow up safely.

Page 21

1. Isabelle greets a chickadee, a swallow, and an oriole.
2. A male red-winged blackbird has black, shiny feathers. He has bright red shoulder patches edged with a thin, yellow stripe. A female has brown feathers with dark streaks.
3. Students' responses will vary. One possible response: Based on information in the story, *camouflage* means "coloring that makes an animal blend into its surroundings."
4. Allow for discussion.

Page 23

1. Cass and Drew live beside the river and visit the manatees on the riverbank.
2. Manatees are endangered by propellers from boats, by fishermen's nets, and by jet skiers.
3. Cass and Drew make signs that read "Slow Down! Manatee Crossing."
4. Allow for discussion.

Page 25

1. When litoi wanders all over the world, he sees birds and other animals, trees, flowers, mountains, valleys, deserts, and streams.
2. litoi creates the butterflies so that the children will be happy even when they are older.
3. Students' responses will vary. One possible response: The Papago probably tell tales like this one to explain how different creatures came to be in the world.
4. Allow for discussion.

Page 27

1. Jack Murphy is the saddest man in Ireland because his crops have failed, his cupboards are empty, his wife has gone home to her mother, and he can't pay the rent.
2. Jack's landlord asks him how much the moon weighs, how many stars sparkle in the night sky, and what he is thinking.
3. Students' responses will vary. One possible response: When Jack looks up at the sky, he sees only a fourth of the moon; four quarter moons equal one whole moon.
4. Students' responses will vary. One possible response: Jack means that he is smarter than his landlord gives him credit for.

Page 29

1. Fisher Bran is unhappy because every day is the same and he has no one to share his life with.
2. Fisher Bran catches a boy while fishing and takes him home. Then he starts teaching the boy the ways of the sea.
3. The child belongs in the sea, and being away from his home makes him sad.
4. Students' responses will vary. One possible response: He is no longer lonely and his days are varied by teaching the children different things.

Page 31

1. The women first go to talk to the mayor because the village is overrun by mice.
2. The mayor brings cats, dogs, bulls, and elephants to the village.
3. Students' responses will vary. One possible response: This story takes place over a year. You can tell by the clothes the women wear and the condition of the road when they go to see the mayor.
4. Students' responses will vary. One possible response: Based on the mayor's solutions throughout the story, the town will probably be overrun again with mice and the whole thing will start over.

Page 33

1. Po Sing's mother wants to explain why she paints the door red for the new year.
2. The old man has observed Nian over the years and noticed the things that frighten him.
3. They wave red banners, light a big bonfire, and explode bamboo tubes.
4. Po Sing's family paints the door red and throws a flashing string of firecrackers out the front door at the stroke of midnight. It is a tradition that is supposed to keep Nian away.

Page 35

1. Lithia Ann is concerned because she has left her needle and thimble at home.
2. The children will tell the authorities that the girls are learning to sew and the boys are learning carpentry.
3. The children are going to the steamboat to learn how to read and write.
4. The children have to hide the fact that they are learning to read and write because it was not legal to educate black people during the time this story takes place.

Page 37

1. The Civil War is being fought.
2. Anna dreams of becoming a soldier. Students' responses to the second part of the question will vary. One possible response: Anna wants to become a soldier because she wants to help her country.
3. Anna always seems to cause trouble because she imagines being a soldier instead of concentrating on what she's doing.
4. Anna brings water to the drummer boy.

Page 39

1. Walt Disney was an imaginative child. He was a dreamer. He liked to doodle in class instead of doing schoolwork.
2. Besides cartoons, Walt Disney created Disneyland.
3. The famous cartoon characters to which this statement refers are Mickey Mouse, Donald Duck, Jiminy Cricket, and Goofy.
4. Allow for discussion.

Page 41

1. This story takes place in the Mauch Chunk mine around 1827.
2. Joseph's and Hiram's fathers work for the Mauch Chunk coal mine. Hiram's father digs coal, and Joseph's father is the brakeman on the Switchback Gravity Railroad.
3. Students' responses will vary. One possible response: The Switchback Gravity Railroad led to the roller coaster.
4. Allow for discussion.

Page 43

1. At the beginning of the story, men come to Samuel's house and force his family to leave its home.
2. The soldiers say that Samuel's family must leave its home because the Cherokees have signed a treaty agreeing to leave.
3. Students' responses will vary. One possible response: The Cherokees probably called this time in history the "trail where they cried" because so many of them died on the forced march to Oklahoma.
4. Allow for discussion.

Page 45

1. Albert wishes that the other kids in the class would notice him.
2. His teacher won't let him jump 20 phone books on his bike at school because he doesn't have any protective gear and she is afraid he might get hurt.
3. Students' responses will vary. One possible response: It is important to Albert that the other kids notice him because he wants to make friends with them.
4. Allow for discussion.

Page 47

1. The assignment is to bring a favorite collection to school and find a creative way to display it.
2. Michael doesn't want to put staples in his underwear, which he would have to do to display it on poster board. Displaying it on hangers seems too boring.
3. Stephen thinks Michael is nuts and that everyone will laugh at him.
4. Students' responses will vary. One possible response: It's a success. Everyone laughs and has fun seeing it, and the teacher says it's the most unusual collection she's ever seen.

Page 49

1. Zoe wears animal slippers to school because they're the closest she can get to having a pet since pets aren't allowed in her apartment building.
2. Zoe brings a snake, a tarantula, a box turtle, a parakeet, a guinea pig, a salamander, a pair of rabbits, three hamsters, a family of white mice, and a bucket of hermit crabs.
3. Students' responses will vary. One possible response: Principal Walden probably doesn't like the zoo because he shouts, "Call an exterminator!"
4. Allow for discussion.

Page 51

1. Zach probably thinks it will be easier to prove his socks are stinky than to write a poem or name all of the capitals of South American countries.
2. The plan is to wear the same socks every day for a week and then take off his shoes in public places and write down whatever comments people make. Students' responses to the second part of the question will vary.
3. Allow for discussion.
4. Allow for discussion.

Page 53

1. Timothy and Tina are twins.
2. The twins' parents don't buy them the toys they want for their birthday because they have some unexpected expenses and can't afford the toys.
3. Students' responses will vary. One possible response: They probably give up their favorite things because they love each other and know how bad it feels not to get what you want for your birthday.
4. Allow for discussion.

Page 55

1. Most of the students in Michael's class collect baseball cards.
2. Students' responses will vary. One possible response: Although one student yawns and Gordy Parker teases Michael, the students in Michael's class probably like his collection. They may talk with him in private just as Patty Mulloni does.
3. Students' responses will vary. One possible response: Michael will probably give the feather to Patty because she gave him two new words for his collection.
4. Allow for discussion.

Page 57

1. Carey is the narrator and Damian is pretending to be the cartoon Tasmanian devil.
2. Real Tasmanian devils are black and furry. They both snarl a lot, and they both have a short tail, a big head, a thick body, and powerful teeth. The cartoon Tasmanian devil is brown and spins around.
3. Carey is talking about the fact that Tasmanian devils are marsupials. The female carries her babies in her pouch and takes care of them until they can take care of themselves.
4. Allow for discussion.

Page 59

1. Students' responses will vary. One possible response: Based on the story, a *herpetologist* is someone who studies reptiles.
2. Nick thinks Monty might be in Hannah's room because she has a gerbil, and Monty might want to eat it.
3. Rupesh puts a book on top of the gerbil cage so that if Monty tries to get into the cage, he won't be able to lift the lid.
4. Allow for discussion.

Page 61

1. Sam is a slow, older dog who usually just lies around in the sun. Seeing him run around in circles seems out of character.
2. Sam is good company, especially in the afternoons before Bruce's mother comes home from work.
3. If Bruce had not followed Sam to his bedroom, he might have been injured by breaking glass when the sliding glass door shattered onto the ottoman where he had been sitting.
4. Students' responses will vary. Possible responses include from his mother, his teacher, or the news media.

Page 63

1. Students' responses will vary. Possible responses: Dana's visitor looks for her missing tooth under her pillow, under her folded clothes, among the stuffed animals stacked on a shelf, in her closet, in her laundry hamper, and in a glass of mouthwash.
2. Students' responses will vary. One possible response: Based on details in the story, Dana is probably a very neat girl who takes good care of her things.
3. Students' responses will vary. One possible response: The tooth fairy probably says that she should have known where Dana put her tooth because a girl who keeps her room so clean would want to keep the tooth clean too.
4. Allow for discussion.

Page 65

1. The story collector is an odd woman who dresses in strange clothes. She claims she writes children's books, but Kateke can't find her books in the library or on any online bookstores. Whenever Kateke's friends tell her one of their stories, the story seems to vanish from their minds.
2. Kateke's mother made more money than the other cab drivers.
3. Kateke's friends don't care enough about the stories they tell to remember them.
4. Students' responses will vary. One possible response: Yes, she will remember because the story is very special to her; it reminds her of everything that makes her mother who she is.

Page 67

1. Kelsey is expecting a big, fire-breathing dragon and Jing-wei is a tiny dragon.
2. Jing-wei plans to have Kelsey do the things to her brother that he has done to her, only better, so that he will understand how it feels and stop bothering her.
3. Jing-wei has to finish the chess game with the emperor.
4. Allow for discussion.

Page 69

1. The parrot steals his mom's diamond earring, and that starts Nelson on his search.
2. Students' responses will vary. One possible response: Nelson wishes he hadn't told the woman about his school's paper drive because she has stacks of newspapers in her apartment that he has to bag up and carry away.
3. Students' responses will vary. One possible response: Based on clues in the story, *pilfering* means "stealing."
4. Allow for discussion.

Page 71

1. Chris doesn't want to leave the beach to go into town because she wants to sketch animal tracks, and she won't have time to do that if they go into town.
2. Tara takes her mother's earring because she wants to make her sand castle special.
3. Students' responses will vary. One possible response: Chris's favorite subject in school is probably science because she likes to study animal tracks, which means she is interested in nature and science.
4. Allow for discussion.

Page 73

1. Chief has never skied before, and her classmates who have are teasing her.
2. Chief's father is a single parent and can't afford skiing trips.
3. Chief smells something hot and metallic.
4. Chief knows a lot about fires since her father is a firefighter. When she sees which way the smoke is blowing, she knows that they will suffocate if they go in that direction.

Page 75

1. Cole has heard stories about high school seniors who rode the coaster into the tunnel and never came out.
2. Not many people are in the park because it is the last weekend before the park closes for the winter and it is cold.
3. Brad is excited about the ride at first, but as they near the river, he gets frightened.
4. Although Cole is afraid of the ride at first, once it is over, he realizes it was fun and he wants to ride it again.